THE GROWTH OF CRIMINAL LAW
IN ANCIENT GREECE

THE
GROWTH OF CRIMINAL LAW
IN ANCIENT GREECE

BY

GEORGE M. CALHOUN

GREENWOOD PRESS, PUBLISHERS
WESTPORT, CONNECTICUT

Library of Congress Cataloging in Publication Data

Calhoun, George Miller, 1886-1942.
  The growth of criminal law in ancient Greece.

  Reprint of the 1927 ed. published by the University
of California Press, Berkeley.
  Bibliography: p.
  1. Criminal law (Greek law)   I. Title.
Law   345'.38   73-10874
ISBN 0-8371-7043-5

Originally published in 1927 by the University of California
Press, Berkeley

Reprinted by Greenwood Press, Inc.

First Greenwood reprinting 1973
Second Greenwood reprinting 1977

Library of Congress catalog card number 73-10874
ISBN 0-8371-7043-5

Printed in the United States of America

TO

PAUL SHOREY

PREFATORY NOTE

The problems with which this volume has to do first aroused my active interest in 1919, when I was studying the history of pleading in Athenian courts. On August 4, 1921, in Cambridge, England, a preliminary statement of conclusions, with brief selections from the text of the first three chapters, was read to a joint meeting of the English Classical Association and the American Philological Association. This was subsequently printed in the *Proceedings of the Classical Association* XVIII (London, 1922), 86–104. Some changes have been made in the passages reprinted from the *Proceedings*, but these are mainly matters of phraseology and do not involve any material departure from my earlier opinions.

The plan of investigation announced at that time has been followed, with only one exception. That exception, however, is important; the promise to include a discussion of the substantive criminal law as it existed in the period of its maturity has not been carried out. This portion of my project has been abandoned because there are many demands upon my time and an adequate study of the substantive criminal law would inevitably drag out over a period of many years. Other tasks which I have undertaken, and have been compelled to put aside until this volume should be complete, cannot now fairly be longer neglected. If some other student of Greek law should enter upon this inviting field, and should find that this book has in some measure cleared the ground for his investigations, I shall feel that my work has not been useless. It has been delightful and fascinating, at every stage, and its completion leaves me vaguely troubled, as one who has long had a safe refuge from petty tribulation and must give up the key.

A number of studies which treat of the Attic criminal law—some of them on my desk as I write—have not been referred to in notes or bibliography, because they merely repeat, without critical consideration, the assumptions whose correctness I am challenging. They are included, in so far as they have come to my attention, in *A Working Bibliography of Greek Law*, (to appear in "Harvard Studies in Legal Bibliography").

In order to guard against a misapprehension that might possibly arise, I may be permitted to disclaim any intention of arguing against the interrelations between law and religion that inevitably exist wherever law and religion stand side by side. I am concerned here, not with sweeping generalities, but with the specific question whether religion, through the doctrine of pollution and the religious aspects of homicide, exerted a preponderant influence upon the growth of criminal law in the Greek city-state. It is my opinion, however, that the influence of ritual and religion upon law was less marked among the Greeks than among many other peoples in comparable stages of development.

The Board of Research of the University of California has placed me under very great obligation by support and encouragement of this investigation at every stage. My colleagues, Professor J. T. Allen, Professor I. M. Linforth, and Professor O. K. McMurray, have kindly read the manuscript and have given me the benefit of their criticism and suggestions. To Professor Roscoe Pound, Dean of the Harvard Law School, my debt is great; for several years his liberal and scholarly interest in my studies has been a distinct inspiration.

To Mr. Joseph W. Flinn, University Printer, my best thanks are due for his generous expenditure of time and energy upon this volume.

Berkeley, California,
January, 1926.

CONTENTS

πάνθ', ὅσα τις βιαζόμενος πράττει, κοίν' ἀδικήματα καὶ κατὰ τῶν ἔξω τοῦ πράγματος ὄντων ἡγεῖθ' ὁ νομοθέτης· τὴν μὲν γὰρ ἰσχὺν ὀλίγων, τοὺς δὲ νόμους ἁπάντων εἶναι, καὶ τὸν μὲν πεισθέντ' ἰδίας, τὸν δὲ βιασθέντα δημοσίας δεῖσθαι βοηθείας.

Demosthenes, xxi. 45.

CHAPTER I

INTRODUCTION

In an independent development from primitive conditions, civil law precedes true criminal law.[1] Considerable progress is made in the maintenance of private rights before the conception of crime as an offense against the social order is consciously formulated, or permanent means established for the legal punishment of such offenses by the community. Thus in Greece what appears to be a well-defined customary procedure for the adjudication of disputes between individuals is found even in the Homeric period.[2] By the time of Hesiod, actual compulsory processes of law for the protection of private rights have made their appearance, antedating by perhaps two hundred years anything which may fairly be called criminal law.[3]

Definitions
of crime

The distinction that is here implied between "criminal law" and "true criminal law" may appear somewhat metaphysical unless certain difficulties of definition are kept in mind. Since criminal law is "that part of the law which relates to crimes and their punishment,"[4] we must begin by

[1] Perrot, *Essai sur le droit public d'Athènes* (Paris, 1869), 330; Maine, *Ancient Law* (Am. ed. 4), 357 ff.

[2] Bonner, "Administration of Justice in the Age of Homer," *Class. Phil.* VI (1911), 12–36; cf. Lipsius, *Das attische Recht und Rechtsverfahren* (Leipzig, 1905–1915), 10; *infra* 17 f.

[3] Bonner, "Administration of Justice in the Age of Hesiod," *Class. Phil.* VII (1912), 17–23; cf. *infra* 30 f.

[4] Stephen, *History of the Criminal Law of England* (London, 1883), I, 1; cf. Bentham, "General View of a Complete Code of Laws," *Works* (Edinburgh, 1843), III, 157.

determining what definition of crime is to be the basis of our investigation. A very slight examination of the various definitions that have been offered will suffice to show that they range from general, theoretical formulas of almost universal validity to others so complex and specialized as to be applicable only to particular legal systems of a rather advanced type. The extremes obviously represent two distinct points of view, neither of which can be disregarded. Thus crime has been defined as a "failure or refusal to live up to the standard of conduct deemed binding by the rest of the community,"[5] as "a revolt of the individual against society,"[6] as "a prohibited action."[7]   If so general a definition as any of these be taken as a criterion, crimes and criminal law are found to have existed in remote ages and in primitive societies.   The first instance, or the first few instances, in which the members of a community united to stone an offender, or to drive him from the village, did not create law; but when it had become the custom so to punish, this custom was criminal law and the acts it punished were crimes.   Each new instance in which the community inflicted punishment either reaffirmed an existing principle or led the way to the establishment of a new one; thus the body of custom having to do with public punishment tended constantly to expand and to become more authoritative.   Here we have the germ of criminal law, primitive and elementary, but none the less law, for it consists of recognized rules of conduct, enforced by the community and involving a punitive sanction.[8]   Yet it is far removed from what the phrase ordinarily connotes.   The theoretical and scientific observer can call it criminal law, because he perceives the thread of

5 Cf. Griffiths in *Encyc. Brit.* VII, 447, *s.v.* "crime."

6 Vinogradoff, *Outlines of Historical Jurisprudence* (London, 1920–1922), I, 35.

7 Bentham, "Principles of Morals and Legislation," *Works* I, 81; cf. also III, 157.

8 See Pollock, *A First Book of Jurisprudence* (London, 1918), chap. 1, "The Nature and Meaning of Law;" cf. also Austin's famous definition of law, and that of Vinogradoff, I, 118 f.

continuity that binds it to the institutions of a later age, or because he has analyzed its logical implications. But what we usually have in mind when we speak of criminal law is something very different from such bits of primordial custom, something which presupposes a fairly advanced condition of society. It is this latter conception of criminal law that is implied in the more complex and particularized definitions of crime found in modern codes and legal treatises.

Our task is twofold. We must look for the appearance of the conception of crime in its simpler and more primitive forms and then study the process of change by which this rudimentary concept becomes more complex and is assimilated more and more to the doctrines that underlie the criminal jurisprudence of modern nations. Hence our inquiry must take account of both types of definition and the concepts for which they stand. We shall employ the one in seeking to identify and select the ideas and practices proper to our subject, and the other in evaluating these data and attempting to determine the stage of development they represent. In thus passing from one aspect of the problem to another, it becomes necessary to distinguish them for the sake of clearness by the use of qualifying expressions, and to speak of "true criminal law," or "criminal law as we understand it," as opposed to elementary and primitive criminal law.[9]

The evolution of
criminal law

Some ideas and institutions seem to be the result of discoveries or inventions that can be definitely attributed to certain times and individuals. Others, like living organisms, clearly owe their existence to a gradual course of evolution; their beginnings are veiled in an obscurity that the most

[9] This distinction is treated from a somewhat different point of view, primarily with reference to Roman law, by Maine, 357 ff. Not all students of the subject, unfortunately, keep it so clearly in mind as does Maine (cf. *infra* 4 f., 13).

painstaking research cannot penetrate, and it is impossible to say when or how they first appeared. We can only study the processes of their development, so far as they are susceptible of observation, in the hope of being able to discern now and again a decisive point at which some essential characteristic is acquired. The ideas with which this study has to do, and the institutions to which they gave rise, manifestly belong to the latter class. We cannot hope to determine the precise moment at which the conception of "crime" as an offense against society first emerges and is consciously differentiated from the broader and more elementary notion of "wrong" or "injury." Nor is it easy to say just when this conception first leads to the appearance of true criminal law. One would have to search very far back indeed to find a society which did not occasionally unite in punishing, either directly or through its leaders, particularly grave or atrocious offenses against the community; and we have remarked that the custom gradually created in this way unquestionably contained the germs of criminal law. Other elements invariably present in a mature system of criminal law have their origin in what may be termed a primitive law of "tort," by which society permits or assists the individual to obtain satisfaction for an invasion of his rights, but without as yet realizing that many such invasions injuriously affect the public welfare and not that of the individual alone.[10] These two groups of ideas and practices are at first distinct and separate, and the appearance of criminal law as we understand it must wait upon their fusion. The notion of a wrong to the com-

---

[10] Throughout this study the word "tort" will be used, not in the technical sense it bears in English law, but with the broader meaning familiar to readers of Maine. The distinction made in the text between "crime" and "tort" is enlarged upon by Maine in his chapter on "Delict and Crime" (358 ff.). In this attempt at analysis, I have chosen to contrast the individual victim, rather than the family, with the community. It must be kept in mind, however, that in primitive societies the rights of individuals are likely to be enforced by action of the family through its head; this will appear from the discussion of Homeric justice (*infra* 16 ff.) and of certain archaic forms of criminal process (*infra* 67 ff.).

munity must be extended to include many acts at first regarded solely as offenses against the individual, and the processes by which the community punishes must be developed and adapted to the adequate protection of all rights, private as well as public, which enter into this enlarged conception of public peace and good order. For the purposes of our inquiry, we may assume that true criminal law, in the usual acceptation of the words, will exhibit three essential characteristics. (1) It will recognize the principle that attacks upon the persons or property of individuals, or rights thereto annexed, as well as offenses that affect the state directly, may be violations of the public peace and good order. (2) It will provide, as part of the ordinary machinery of government, means by which such violations may be punished by and for the state, and not merely by the individual who may be directly affected. (3) The protection it offers will be readily available to the entire body politic, and not restricted to particular groups or classes of citizens.[11]

The general processes by which true criminal law is evolved from primitive beginnings are found to be much the same in various instances. On the other hand, the particular institutions to which they give rise naturally differ according to the character of the society in question, its cultural contacts and traditions, forms of government, and other determining influences that are likely to be both numerous and complex. In Rome, for example, the criminal jurisdiction directly exercised in early times by the *comitia* gradually came to be entrusted to *quaestiones* or commissions. At first special commissions were convened for the punishment of particular acts, but at a later time statutes were passed

[11] In the interest of clearness, it must be noted that the presence in the territory of the state of slaves, who derive little or no protection from the law, or of aliens, whose rights are often not adequately protected, does not enter into consideration here. Ancient criminal law must of course be evaluated upon the basis of the ancient theory of the state. For examples of criminal law and process available only to privileged classes of citizens, cf. *infra* 52 f., 82 f.

defining certain acts as crimes and creating permanent commissions with authority to punish them whenever they might
be committed. This last step, the institution of the *quaestiones perpetuae* in the second century B.C., in Maine's
opinion, marks the emergence of true criminal law in Rome.[12]

*Emergence of true
criminal law in Greece*

Our knowledge of the administration of justice in Greece
goes back—thanks to the Homeric poems—to a time when
offenses against individuals or family groups were still dealt
with mainly by self-help, while flagrant attacks upon the
community were punished by direct and spontaneous action
of the populace that was little more than mob action.[13] In
the seventh century B.C. in Athens offenses against the state
were punished as crimes by the aristocratic council, and
attacks upon individuals were dealt with as torts through
proceedings instituted by the aggrieved person before a
magistrate.[14] The decisive step in the transition to true
criminal law seems to have been taken in Athens at the
beginning of the sixth century. At that time Solon, we are
told, gave to every citizen a right of action in the prosecution of certain offenses, including attacks upon individuals
as well as upon the state.[15] Here, apparently, begins the
fusion of the two primitive methods of punishing the various
acts we now regard as crimes. Invasions of individual rights
that have hitherto been dealt with exclusively as torts have,
in some instances at least, come to be regarded as crimes,
creating a right of action in the whole body politic; at the

[12] 378 ff.; cf. Stephen I, 11 f.; for a different opinion regarding the origin of the
quaestiones, cf. Strachan-Davidson, *Problems of the Roman Criminal Law* (Oxford,
1912), I, 131 ff.; II, 16 ff.

[13] *Infra* 20 ff.

[14] *Infra* 52 f., 61 f.

[15] Ar. *Cons. Ath.* ix. 1; cf. Plut. *Solon* xviii. See Linforth, "Solon the Athenian,"
Univ. Calif. Publ. Class. Phil. VI (Berkeley, 1919), 87. On the various offenses
dealt with by Solon, cf. *infra* 81 ff.

same time the simple procedure of the old law of tort is applied to the punishment of crime, making it possible for any citizen who may wish to do so to act as prosecutor and thus give effect to the public right of action. This type of criminal action, in which the initiation of prosecution is left to the individual citizen and not entrusted to a public functionary, was the one most generally prescribed in subsequent criminal legislation in Athens; consequently the Attic criminal law, like the English, was essentially litigious rather than inquisitorial.[16]

*Problems
involved*

Here unquestionably we are face to face with a great event. For the first time in the history of the Western world, a political government has by its enactments defined crime somewhat as it is defined today, and has provided machinery for the punishment of crimes by the body politic. Many questions of deep import suggest themselves. Was the act of Solon the conscious application of a doctrine of crime? If so, what was that doctrine, and how did it develop? Was it original with Solon, or can we discern its gradual unfolding in the political thought of prior generations? What were the immediate purposes of the enactment? What social and economic conditions was it designed to meet? Did it lead to the orderly and rational development of a scientific criminal jurisprudence, or was it merely the beginning of a series of random accretions comparable to the multiplication of the *quaestiones* in Rome?

If we seek for answers to these queries in our handbooks and special studies, or in our histories, we shall be disappointed. Unfortunately we have to do with that obscure period between the eighth and fifth centuries for which

---

[16] On the English criminal law, cf. Stephen I, 506 f.; on the general characteristics of Athenian criminal law and procedure, cf. *infra* 129 ff.; Vinogradoff II, 165 ff.

authentic sources of information are but few. Thonissen, whose *Droit pénal de la république athénienne* has been the standard work of reference in this field for the past fifty years, frankly professes inability to deal with this period. What is more, he bluntly asserts that the detailed history of the successive modifications in the criminal law of Athens "ne sera jamais écrite."[17] Those who have been less diffident have for the most part attempted to meet the difficulty by following deductive rather than inductive methods, and their results smack of the metaphysical. The investigator constructs an ideal state; he traces its colorless progress from the primitive monarchy to democracy, and as part of that progress depicts the evolution of a criminal law. He quotes freely from authors who wrote centuries afterward all that lends itself to his particular theory, and too often is but slightly concerned with the little definite, contemporary information we do possess in regard to political and economic conditions. No one, apparently, has deemed it worth while to ask why Solon should have introduced this particular innovation at this particular juncture; it seems to be taken for granted, when Solon is mentioned at all, that it was "in the air," that Athens had reached a stage in the evolution of human institutions at which something of the sort was to be expected.[18] On the other hand, a disproportionate emphasis upon the history of homicide conveys the impression that the whole evolution of law in Hellas was determined

---

[17] *Le droit pénal de la république athénienne* (Brussels and Paris, 1875), p. iv. It is true that Thonissen had in mind primarily the substantive law, rather than courts and procedure; but it will appear from the following pages how intimately the former subject is bound up with the latter and how much can be gleaned from a careful study of the sources.

[18] Lipsius, *Recht*, 31; Thonissen, 76 ff.; Glotz, *La solidarité de la famille dans le droit criminel en Grèce* [Paris, 1904], 369 ff.; this last account is by far the most adequate and thoughtful. Gilliard (*Quelques réformes de Solon* [Lausanne, 1907], 290) apparently makes the mistake of thinking that only actions against magistrates are involved. Freeman (*The Work and Life of Solon* [London, 1926], 132) characterizes Solon's innovation as "an advance towards the attitude of the civilized community."

by the treatment of this offense at various times. It is assumed that, when the idea of pollution became attached to the shedding of human blood, the state intervened in the punishment of homicide in order to protect the community from the consequences to which it would be exposed if the proper lustrations were not performed, and this is the decisive step in the evolution of criminal law. To put it more concisely and concretely, one who seeks information will find a great deal on the history of homicide—much of it a projection backwards in time of material found in the orators, or even later writers. He will find little or nothing on the conception of crime or true criminal law.[19]

The "Blutgerichte"
theory

The theories to which I refer rest upon the assumption—which has gone practically unchallenged for at least a century—that the Greeks normally looked upon the taking of human life as a crime, that their actions for homicide were criminal actions, their laws on the punishment of homicide criminal law. Meier, who followed out this principle consistently, not only included the various homicide actions among the "öffentliche Klagen," but even went so far as to enter them in his index as γραφαί and not δίκαι, calmly disregarding the unvarying usage of classical writers.[20] Thonissen likewise calls them γραφαί, remarking that they are

[19] The fairness of this criticism can be tested only by consulting the various studies and handbooks to which reference is made in the following chapters. For example, Glotz's exhaustive and erudite volume *La solidarité de la famille*, though it is filled with important and interesting information, tells us little or nothing of the gradual growth of the conception of crime as distinguished from tort. Contemporary sources have been too much neglected by students of this difficult period, who place their reliance mainly in documents of much later date. Thonissen (*introd.*, p. v) complains that some fragments of Solon's laws are the only authentic sources, and that many of these are open to suspicion. He ignores utterly the poems; these, and not the so-called laws of Solon, are the truly authentic documents, as Linforth (4 ff.) properly points out.

[20] Meier and Schoemann, *Der attische Process* (Halle, 1824). Cf. the same work, revised by Lipsius (Berlin, 1883–1887), 376 ff., 618 ff.

incontestably to be classed as public actions.[21] Lipsius, in *Attisches Recht*, reinstates them among the "Privatklagen," but the change is merely one of formal classification. He infers from their inclusion among the δίκαι, not that Meier's position is unsound, and the Athenians associated them with the private rather than the public actions, but that the Athenians were not very clear upon the distinction between criminal and civil law.[22] Philippi takes for granted that they are criminal actions, and describes them as the most important exception to the rule that a criminal prosecution may be instituted by any citizen; this exceptional characteristic is a survival from the blood feud.[23] When one has followed this topic through the various handbooks and special studies, he is not surprised that Leist founds his exhaustive study of the origins of criminal law[24] upon this same assumption, and centers his whole account in the development of the *Blutgerichte*: "Der Mord und die Frage seiner Bestrafung durch den Tod wird immer das Centrum des Criminalrechts sein."[25] "Die Tödtungsfrage ist die nahezu wichtigste aller Rechtsfragen. Bei ihr hat sich die Menschheit zuerst an Prüfung des Gegensatzes von Gut und Böse, von Recht und Unrecht gemacht. Deshalb ist in ihrem Gebiete auch das etwa älteste Stück der Rechtsgeschichte zu suchen."[26] It is hard to understand how one could have written these words after reading the Homeric poems, our greatest and practically our earliest source for Aryan tribal institutions. Even Glotz, who is well aware that the δίκαι φονικαί were not criminal actions, with all his acumen and his encyclopaedic learning, is distinctly under the sway of the prevailing idea.[27]

The most perfunctory glance at the primary sources must evoke grave suspicions regarding the soundness of this

[21] 80, n. 2.   [22] *Recht*, 242 ff.   [23] *Der Areopag und die Epheten* (Berlin, 1874), 68 ff.
[24] *Gräco-italische Rechtsgeschichte* (Jena, 1884), 286–423.
[25] *Ibid*. 379.   [26] *Ibid*. 423.   [27] 372 ff., 227 ff.

premise. (In the Homeric poems, as we shall see, homicide is a simple wrong against the individual or the family; it is not looked upon as morally reprehensible, or as an offense against the common welfare.[28]) The writers of the classical period invariably speak of the homicide actions as δίκαι, the generic term for private suits, and never as γραφαί.[29] These suits lack the one essential mark of the criminal action, the vesting of the right of action in the whole body politic. They were never entirely assimilated to the γραφή, but were at most a quasi-criminal form.[30] (It would be difficult indeed to justify the logic which seeks the origin of criminal law in such an action. Nothing could be more irrational than the assumption that the treatment of homicide, which remained for centuries almost totally unaffected by the development of criminal law and procedure, was the principal operating cause in that development.[31] If any conclusion regarding the influence of religion and ritual upon law is to be drawn from the homicide actions, it would seem to be that this influence is distinctly conservative and tends to retard development. Not a few of the errors which have crept into our attempted reconstructions of ancient life result from the intrusion of modern preconceptions, and one could scarcely cite a more striking example of such wandering from the path of true induction than this, the universal tendency to view the actions for homicide as criminal actions and to see in the law of homicide the nucleus of criminal law.

[28] *Infra* 16 ff.

[29] Cf. Lipsius, *Recht*, 243, n. 13.

[30] On the classification of actions as criminal and quasicriminal, cf. *infra* 129 ff.

[31] Cf. Glotz, 372 ff. Glotz himself believes (400) that the religious aspects of the homicide action are the cause of the failure to assimilate it to the criminal action in Attic law. Apparently he does not perceive how incompatible is this circumstance with his general view of the rise of criminal justice, and he is at no pains in his account to establish a connection between the hypothetical influence of religion and the political and social ideas of Solon.

Scope and method
of this inquiry

With the hope of being able here and there to illuminate these interesting problems by a ray of new light, I propose to follow out several fairly definite lines of inquiry. The first will have to do with the evolution of the conception of crime and with the attitude assumed by the community or the state in different periods toward homicide and other acts that are now regarded as crimes. Here it will be advisable to study our sources in chronological order, so far as may be possible, and to be on our guard against the intrusion of ideas whose existence cannot be actually demonstrated from the texts of the period under discussion. Secondly, an attempt will be made to relate Solon's institution of criminal prosecutions definitely to the gradual evolution of a doctrine of crime and to specific problems that confronted him in his task of reconstituting the state. In this connection, attention will be invited to some implications of the Athenian legal vocabulary which have not hitherto been studied as thoroughly as their importance merits. In the third place, I shall endeavor to trace the history of Athenian criminal legislation after Solon in the light of what is known regarding social and political conditions in Attica at various times. This will be followed by a chapter, necessarily brief and incomplete, on the state of the criminal law in Crete and in other Hellenic states, and by a few observations on the general character of the Attic criminal law in the fifth and fourth centuries. Inasmuch as the inquiry is concerned primarily with the general evolution of criminal law and procedure, no attempt will be made to present a systematic exposition of the substantive law, or to discuss the history of specific offenses and their punishment.

Crime and
tort

The objection may be made that the distinction I have emphasized between crime and tort is largely a matter of terminology. The early history of crime, it will be urged, is invariably merged in that of tort, and the precise moment at which the conception of crime first appears distinctly and begins to influence legislation is of slight importance in comparison with the long period during which many wrongs that we now regard as crimes were dealt with as torts; the evolution of this primitive law of tort and its contribution to criminal law may have been materially affected by the treatment of homicide and in particular by the doctrine of pollution. This last possibility we shall find it advisable to keep carefully in mind throughout the earlier chapters. But the general objection, which proposes in effect that we take a modern conception of crime as the starting point for an investigation into the notions of the ancient Hellenes, I cannot approve. The only possible way to discover what was the primitive conception of crime, to trace its development and compare it with our own, is to ascertain what offenses were punished by the united action of the community, and to distinguish them from those which were left to be dealt with by the individual or the family. In general we may say that an offense which society is accustomed to punish, at first by direct action of the populace, later by some form of public action at law, is at the time regarded as a crime. The failure to keep this necessary distinction in mind has long prevented us from forming a just idea of Greek criminal law or fully understanding the processes by which it was evolved from primitive custom.

Again, the reader may feel that the discussions of social and political problems in some of the earlier chapters are out of proportion in a study of this kind. In general, however, I believe they have not been allowed to exceed what is indispensable to the prosecution of the inquiry. Where they enter into detail, as in the account of pre-Solonian political conditions, they profess to extend, or at least make more precise, our knowledge of matters inseparable from the history of criminal legislation. To borrow the admirable language of Sir James Stephen,[32] in the preface to his great work on the criminal law of England, this portion of the study is "longer and more elaborate than I originally meant it to be, but, until I set myself to study the subject as a whole, and from the historical point of view, I had no idea of the way in which it connected itself with all the most interesting parts of . . . . history, and it has been matter of unceasing interest to see how the crude, imperfect definitions . . . . were gradually moulded . . . . and how the clumsy institutions . . . . gradually grew into a body of courts and a course of procedure. . . . ."

[32] I, p. viii.

CHAPTER II

THE HOMERIC AGE

The student of legal history who has attempted to reconstruct early Roman law from the scattered hints that are his sole dependence, or to separate from Roman and Christian accretions what is indigenous in the Germanic codes, will have cause to congratulate himself when he comes to study the beginnings of Greek political life. In the Homeric poems he will have the fullest and most ancient tradition of primitive life and custom among the Indo-European peoples. The social and political usages of the tribal group are still clearly visible in the rudimentary city-state, and the scenes successively presented to his view embrace what was then the whole field of human activity. The *Iliad* and the *Odyssey* are indeed our first and greatest body of evidence for the early history of European institutions, the proper starting point for any historical inquiry into the life and thought of the western world.[1]

The general course which the evolution of criminal law may be expected to follow has been traced. Our problem now is to determine what degree of progress the practices depicted in the Homeric poems represent, and in so doing to discover, if possible, the general character of the ideas which have given rise to these practices and are likely to influence their future development. Perhaps as good a way as any to approach the subject will be to inquire how the

---

[1] Maine, with his usual acumen, was among the first to perceive the peculiar importance of the Homeric poems in the study of institutions. As he points out (2 f.), the very fact that the matters with which we have to do "were not yet the subjects of conscious observation" when the poems were composed, enables us to put greater reliance on the information they contain.

Greeks of the Homeric age deal with the various wrongs that are now regarded as crimes. What offenses, if any, does the community unite in repressing? Which are left to be dealt with by the individual or the family? Which are coming to be consciously regarded as injuries to the general welfare, but are not yet habitually punished by concerted action? It will be well to begin with homicide, since we have questioned the correctness of the view that criminal law in its earlier stages centers in the treatment of this offense.

*Homicide and the
primitive law of tort*

It is now generally agreed that the Homeric epic knows nothing of the doctrine that the shedding of human blood involves pollution, or of lustral rites for homicides.[2] This view does not rest exclusively upon the silence of the sources; to be convinced of its truth one need only consider attentively the Theoclymenus episode in the *Odyssey*, or a number of other passages whose tone is quite incompatible with the ideas of a later age.[3] Nor is any distinction to be observed

---

[2] Bonner, *Class. Phil.* VI, 14 ff.; Glotz, 228 ff.; Thonissen, 44, n. 3; Seymour, *Life in the Homeric Age* (New York, 1907), 88; Philippi, 5, n. 8; Lipsius, *Recht*, 9, n. 25. The opposite view (Müller, *Eumeniden*, 134 ff.) is not now seriously entertained. Further references to discussions of the subject will be found in Glotz, *loc. cit.*, and the evidence has recently been reviewed afresh by M. M. Gillies ("Purification in Homer," *Class. Quar.* XIX [1925], 71–74), who concludes that "we must not interpret purification in Homer in the light of later beliefs; it is inspired solely by a proper and sanitary striving after cleanliness." The whole subject of homicide in ancient Hellas has recently been studied at great length by Treston in *Poine. A Study in Ancient Greek Blood-Vengeance* (London, 1923). The author starts with Leaf's theory of an Achaean aristocracy ruling over a Pelasgian population, and attempts, by arguments which I find more ingenious than convincing, to show that two modes of dealing with homicide existed side by side in Homeric times, a Pelasgian tribal system of wergeld and an Achaean blood-feud regulated by "a kind of social etiquette or a potential military discipline" (423). Treston admits that "purgation for homicide was unknown to the Greeks of Homeric times" (112).

[3] The Theoclymenus episode should be studied in its entirety (*Odyssey* xv. 223 ff., 508 ff.; xvii. 71 ff.; xx. 350 ff.); especially notable is the kindly reception on board the ship of a slayer who comes red-handed, openly avowing his act, at the very moment of prayer and libation (*ibid.* xv. 256 ff.). Other instances are cited by Glotz, 229 f.

between premeditated and unintentional or justifiable slaying.[4] All homicides are dealt with by the relatives of the victim, who have no means of obtaining vengeance other than self-help.[5] The blood feud is an established institution, and has reached the stage in which the acceptance of blood-money frequently takes the place of vengeance. If the offense is not atoned in this way, the homicide commonly goes into exile in order to escape death at the hands of the victim's family. Although the slaying of a parent or of a guest meets with general condemnation, "there is no indication of any popular sentiment against ordinary homicide;"[6] it is apparently the violation of the sacred bond with parent or guest, and not the mere taking of human life, that arouses reprobation.[7] In fact the question of right and wrong seems not to have entered into the Homeric feeling toward homicide, even though the act be committed under circumstances that would today stamp it as a brutal murder.[8]

Other attacks upon the persons or property of individuals of the sort which are now very generally punished as crimes seem uniformly to have been left to the individual to deal with as he might see fit with the aid of his family.[9]

It would be a mistake to infer from this inattention to the moral and social aspects of homicide and other acts of violence that the Greeks of the Homeric age have not their notions of right and justice. In fact, means have been devised for deciding disputes between individuals in accordance with these notions. The person who does not wish to

---

[4] Glotz, 48 ff.; Bonner, *Class. Phil.* VI, 19; Philippi, 4 ff.; Lipsius, *Recht*, 7, 601, n. 4. The erroneous reasoning of Leist, who maintains the opposite view (329 ff.), is noticed by Lipsius, *loc. cit.* Treston (52 ff.) attempts to show that the Pelasgians made distinctions of this sort.

[5] On the blood-feud, composition, and exile, in Homeric times, cf. Bonner, 16 ff.; Glotz, 47 ff., 94 ff.; *Recht*, 7 f.; Seymour, 88 ff. Treston devotes many pages to these subjects (especially 23–77).

[6] Bonner, 15 f.; cf. Seymour, *loc. cit.*

[7] *Odyssey* xxi. 27 ff.

[8] *Odyssey* xiii. 267 ff., with Bonner's comment (15).

[9] Bonner, 19 ff.; Thonissen, 45 ff.

resort to force in order to assert his right may challenge his opponent to refer their difference for arbitration to prominent members of the community, usually gerontes or elders, or even to the king. How well established the practice of voluntary arbitration has become is shown by constant allusions to these quasi-judicial functions of the kings and elders.[10] In the trial scene from the shield of Achilles,[11] our only detailed description of such an arbitration, the proceedings have their origin in a homicide. The elders, in their seats of smooth-hewn stone in the crowded assembly-place, are deciding between two men who dispute regarding the blood-price of a man slain; the one claims that he has paid the price in full, the other asserts that he has not received it at all. The folk are greatly excited, shouting for one or the other of the disputants, and the heralds who attend upon the elders keep order while the latter rise one after another and give their opinions. The homicide itself is not in issue; the question before the "court" has to do solely with the payment of the blood-price, and has been voluntarily submitted to arbitration exactly as any other private and personal difference might have been submitted.

In only one instance, I believe, do the foregoing statements involve questions which are still the subject of serious controversy. The opinion is often advanced that in the trial scene the issue is not whether the blood-price has been paid, but whether it must be accepted or may be refused. This view, if it be correct, would imply that the homicide is in some way in issue, and not merely the fact of payment. The question cannot be absolutely decided either one way

---

[10] For example, Iliad i. 238 f.: δικασπόλοι, οἵ τε θέμιστας πρὸς Διὸς εἰρύαται; cf. Odyssey xi. 186; iii. 244; Iliad xvi. 542. According to Treston, the "Pelasgian" tribal elders have the work and worry of judicial duties, while the "Achaean" lords reap the glory and shamelessly wear the titles. "The Elders," he says (89), "are . . . . the real δικασπόλοι βασιλεῖς of the Homeric society. The fact that the Achaean kings are credited with this title in Homer does not prove that they ever functioned as such." This is a very fair specimen of Treston's manner of interpreting his sources.

[11] Iliad xviii. 497 ff.; cf. Bonner 24 ff.

or the other. I am inclined to favor the older and simpler interpretation in which the question is merely whether or not the blood-money has been paid.[12] However, I may be permitted to observe that, even if we regard the homicide as the issue, the passage affords no ground for the belief that homicide was in any way set apart from other offenses. The reference to arbitration is clearly voluntary, and there is of course no hint of pollution or purification.

So far we have found not the slightest warrant for assuming that the feeling of the Homeric Greeks toward homicide, as distinguished from other acts of violence, or their methods of dealing with the offense, exercised any particular influence in the direction of a theory of crime and punishment. It is quite obvious that the doctrine of pollution and the cathartic ceremonies to which it gave rise could have had nothing to do with the development of criminal law in a society for which they did not exist. Nor is there any reason to believe that homicide, more than other offenses, directed men's thoughts toward the problem of crime in a time when it was not particularly associated with questions of right and wrong, or looked upon as a menace to the general well-being of society. In point of procedure it is squarely upon a footing with other attacks upon individuals, which are left for the individual or the family to redress. Disputes arising from homicides must in the nature of things have been numerous in these early times, but they are evidently not distinguished in any way from other disputes and are adjusted by voluntary arbitration. So far is the offense, apparently, from being a cause of the first attempts at application of the

[12] The more important discussions of this problem, which has become the central point in a dispute that bids fair to prove interminable, are cited by Glotz, 115 ff., and Bonner, *loc. cit.* Since the words of the poet might conceivably be used in either sense, it seems unlikely that the question can ever be positively answered one way or the other. In my opinion the objections to the earlier interpretation have been sufficiently answered by Glotz and Bonner. According to Treston (33 ff., 88 ff.) the trial-scene presents a "Pelasgian" court, of whose activities the "Achaeans" knew little and cared less.

principles of right and order, that in the trial scene just described, the sole instance in the poems in which we see a homicide in the process of adjudication, the matter comes before the "court" only at a stage when the question at issue is no longer the slaying but merely the payment of the blood-price. One is tempted to conclude that the earliest attempts to apply notions of justice grew out of disputes between individuals or families over *rights* or *property*, and acts of violence were at first matters for adjudication only when translated into questions of this sort. There is certainly no reason to believe that homicide exerted any preponderant influence even upon the primitive law of tort which is the precursor of true criminal law.[13]

The beginnings
of criminal law

If we look in quite another direction, however, we shall be able to discern the faint foreshadowings of a doctrine of crime, and even sporadic cases in which society, not merely the individual or the family, seeks to inflict punishment. The good and the bad actions of men are coming to be comprehended under general concepts, and these concepts are sometimes expressed in terms which show that the maintenance of the social order has been taken into account in their formation. Thus in the *Odyssey* the good and the evil aspects of human activity are contrasted in the antithesis of ὕβρις and εὐνομίη—the gods in divers guise haunt the cities of earth and observe alike the wanton violence and the good

---

[13] Here it may be objected that the very appearance of composition is a first step toward the recognition of the criminal character of homicide, and evinces an awakening desire to guard the public peace and well-being against the disorders involved in private or family vengeance. We need not inquire into the origins of the practice (studied exhaustively by Glotz, chap. 4), or the possibility that at this time the composition was still little more than a ransom, or the commutation of death or exile. It will suffice to point out that the practice is not peculiar to homicide; it is found in the Homeric poems in connection with other offenses, notably adultery (*Odyssey* viii. 332; cf. 353, 355 ff.), and may quite as well have had its origin in the one class of cases as the other.

order of mankind.[14] In the same poem is a picture of the
"god-fearing" monarch (θεουδής) who upholds right and
justice (εὐδικίαι), for whom the fields and flocks and even the
sea bring forth in plenty, all in consequence of his "good
leadership" (ἐξ εὐηγεσίης), and the people prosper under his
sway.[15] These notions are not restricted to the *Odyssey*.
In the *Iliad* the poet describes the tempestuous fury of Zeus,
when he is filled with rage at men who bring force into the
gathering-place of the folk and decree "crooked dooms" and
drive out justice, recking not of the vengeance of the gods.[16]
With this may be compared Nestor's words, "friendless,
lawless, homeless, is he who doth long for the horrors of civil
strife."[17]

Other passages contain allusions to particular acts that
threaten the general security and well-being. Hector,
reproaching Paris for the action that is to bring about the
extinction of his race, concludes "truly are the Trojans
cowards, else hadst thou ere this put on a tunic of stones for
the great evil thou hast wrought."[18] In Ithaca Eupithes,
for an act which aroused the anger of a friendly community
and exposed his own folk to the danger of reprisals, came
near to being the victim of just such summary punishment
at the hands of the populace. He was saved only by the
personal intercession of the king, Odysseus, in whose palace
he had sought refuge from the mob.[19] Again, after the
slaying of the suitors, a majority of the Ithacans rush to
arms and attempt to punish Odysseus;[20] this was no ordinary
homicide to be dealt with between family and family, but a
slaughter which took its toll from every notable household
in Ithaca. It is worth noting in this last instance that the
"armed pursuit" is preceded by debate in the assembly, and
the opening speech against Odysseus describes his act as a

---

[14] *Odyssey* xvii. 485–88. [17] *Ibid.* ix. 63–64. [19] *Odyssey* xvi. 424 ff.
[15] *Ibid.* xix. 109–14. [18] *Ibid.* iii. 56–57. [20] *Ibid.* xxiv. 413 ff.
[16] *Iliad* xvi. 386–88.

great offense, which touches even neighboring communities as well as Ithaca.[21] The possibility of summary action against Agamemnon for his breach of the relation that should obtain between king and people in a well-ordered community is hinted at by Achilles,[22] and later echoed by Thersites, who states explicitly the principle of good order that the king has transgressed: "it beseems thee not, being the leader, to bring the Achaeans into misfortune."[23]

These are coherent notions and practices, whose sum gives a fairly definite outline. There is a distinct feeling that justice, good order, good government, are essential to the general well-being, and their opposites invite disaster. The perversion of justice and the stirring up of internecine strife are offenses which concern the whole community; acts that threaten the general security and well-being are viewed with distinct reprobation. Punishment may come from the gods and also from men. In the case of extraordinary offenses, or acts of which the disastrous consequences to the community are immediately manifest, the populace rises in its anger to inflict summary punishment upon the offender; in at least one instance the "armed pursuit" is preceded by discussion.

It can scarcely be a mere coincidence that the conditions we here behold in actual existence suggest at once Maine's reconstruction of the first and most primitive state of criminal jurisprudence among the Romans. "It is not to be supposed," he says, "that a conception so simple and elementary as that of wrong done to the State was wanting in any primitive society. . . . . When the Roman com-

---

[21] *Odyssey* xxiv. 420–29. The impelling motive of Eupithes is of course the desire for vengeance on the slayer of his son, as appears from the latter part of his harangue, where his feelings get the upper hand. But he skilfully represents the act of Odysseus, not as a matter for merely private revenge, but as a wrong to the whole community, and even brings up against him the fate of the men who had followed the king to Troy. Here we have a striking foreshadowing of the curious mingling of judicial, political, and personal considerations found in political accusations of the fifth and fourth centuries in Athens.

[22] *Iliad* i. 231–32.   [23] *Ibid.* ii. 233 ff.

munity conceived itself to be injured, the analogy of a personal wrong received was carried out to its consequences
with absolute literalness, and the State avenged itself by a
single act on the individual wrongdoer."[24]   After observing
that "the notion of injury to the community" is not found
in "the earliest interference of the State *through its tribunals*,"[25] he goes on, "Nothing . . . . can be simpler than the
considerations which ultimately led ancient societies to the
formation of a true criminal jurisprudence.   The State conceived itself to be wronged, and the Popular Assembly
struck straight at the offender with the same movement
that accompanied its legislative action."[26]   It is significant
that the conclusions derived from a study of the Homeric
poems accord so completely with those suggested to Maine
by his attempts to analyze the earlier stages of the Roman
criminal law.   In Homeric times community action is still
practically mob action; in only one instance is there a
suggestion of deliberation, and anything that may be called
legislation lies in the distant future.   But we have before us,
clear and distinct, what was to develop the εἰσαγγελία and
the προβολή of Athens and the *quaestiones* of Rome, and in
both cases to lead ultimately to true criminal law.

The facts comprehended in this brief account of Homeric
justice are of course familiar to all students of the poems.
Their full implication, however, has not always been perceived, chiefly as a result of the failure of which I have
spoken, to distinguish between the primitive law of tort and
of crime.   We must not be misled by the fewness of the
instances, for the poet does not go out of his way to give a
picture of his times.[27]   Thus, in appraising the progress that
has been made toward an administration of civil justice,
one might form a very erroneous idea were it not for the
description of the shield.   This is an artistic device pure and
simple; yet among the typical scenes from the life of a

[24] 360.   [25] 362.   [26] 368.   [27] Scott, *Homer and His Influence* (Boston, 1925), 28.

Homeric community the arbitration in the assembly-place stands prominently forward. It is worth noting also that in two instances the ideas with which our inquiry is concerned furnish material for similes and therefore cannot be regarded as uncommon or exceptional.[28] Again, the words Hector uses of death by stoning—to "put on a tunic of stones" (λάϊνον ἕσσο χιτῶνα)—are a grim bit of primordial "slang" which could only have developed in a society where this mode of summary execution was a familiar custom.[29] And we have seen that such custom is the first and most elementary stage of criminal law as distinguished from the early law of tort. We may safely conclude that the first hesitating steps in the way which leads eventually to true criminal law were taken by the Greeks as early as the Homeric Age; that the underlying causes have no particular connection with homicide, and certainly none with the doctrine of pollution. If that doctrine has really had any influence upon the evolution of law, we must look for it in the post-Homeric period.

[28] *Odyssey* xix. 109 ff.; *Iliad* xvi. 386 ff.

[29] *Iliad* iii. 56 f. A few centuries ago, when a gibbet stood at every cross-road in England, the language was rich in cant terms for this mode of execution. For some choice specimens, most of them now quite unintelligible, cf. Farmer-Henley, *A Dictionary of Slang and Colloquial English* (London, 1912), 312, *s.v.* "Nubbing-cheat."

CHAPTER III

THE AGE OF HESIOD AND THE LYRIC POETS

Regarded as a source of information, the Homeric literature presents many lacunae, and the student is discouraged at the array of problems that must be left unsolved. Yet, as he reads and rereads, he gets a picture that is fairly complete in its larger outlines and not altogether without detail; he can feel that he really knows something of the Homeric Greeks, their life and their ideas. When he has left behind him the age of epic, however, he must grope in darkness, with only occasional faint flickerings of light from mutilated and scattered sources,[1] until he comes to the beginnings of the classic period and can see once more with some distinctness the objects of his pursuit. Then he finds that the conditions whose emergence he has set himself to trace are already in existence. Athens has developed a doctrine of crime and with it a system of criminal law and procedure. The idea of pollution and the practice of lustration have become associated with the shedding of human blood, and tribunals have been established for dealing with homicides of various sorts.[2] The assumed interrelation between these two sets of facts, the possibility that the former is a development from the latter, must be tested for this obscure period, as best may be, by scrupulous sifting of the literary remains.

[1] Cf. Thonissen, p. iv.
[2] *Recht*, 121 ff., 600 ff.

The doctrine
of pollution

It is quite likely that the idea of pollution was beginning to make its appearance by the eighth century. Otherwise it would be difficult to explain how it had come to be so universally disseminated and so thoroughly invested with an aspect of extreme antiquity in the time of Aeschylus. I cannot, however, believe that the doctrine was already widely prevalent among the Greeks in the age of Hesiod.[3] That poet's account of the slaying of Molurus and the slayer's reception by Orchomenus, though but a fragment, is filled with the spirit of the older epic.[4] In the *Shield*, which is probably post-Hesiodic, the entertainment of Amphitryon in Thebes as an honored guest, with the gracious hospitality that custom prescribes toward suppliants, is a picture from the heroic age.[5] Either scene might well stand side by side with the Theoclymenus episode in the *Odyssey*,[6] and either accords but ill with Glotz's tragic delineation of the fleeing homicide of a later age, a polluted outcast, shunned by citizen and stranger, whose only desire is to hide his disgrace in solitude or in a far country where his antecedents are unknown.[7] Either the doctrine of pollution was not widely prevalent in the society for which these poems were composed, or the poets are archaizing, deliberately and with consummate art. Even though we adopt the latter alternative, we feel that a tremendous gulf separates the thought of this age from that of Aeschylus, when the doctrine of pollution was looked upon as the common heritage of the Hellenes from a remote antiquity.

[3] Cf. Bonner, *Class. Phil.* VII, 22.   [4] *Fr.* 144 (Rzach).

[5] Lines 11 ff., 80 ff. The displeasure of the gods alluded to here has clearly nothing in common with the divine retribution that was later thought to follow spontaneously and almost mechanically upon pollution. It is rather to be compared with the anger the gods of Homer feel toward a homicide under certain aggravating circumstances, e.g., *Odyssey* i. 32 ff., xxi. 27 ff.; *Iliad* ix. 565 ff.

[6] *Supra* 16.   [7] 232.

I am well aware that such statements as these must seem incredible to anyone who is familiar with the traditional view. Discussions of this period give the impression that the doctrine of pollution was its one dominant idea, a compelling, resistless force that controlled the individual and the collective will, moulded judicial and political thought, and left its imperishable stamp upon the literature.[8] Let us turn our attention, however, to the actual evidence on which this impressive picture rests. The details which are sketched in with such profusion are invariably drawn from Aeschylus, Antiphon, Demosthenes, or from even later writers.[9] When the notions for which there is no evidence earlier than the fifth or fourth centuries are cleared away, there is disclosed, as the groundwork for this imposing fabric of conjecture, either the assertion that Hesiod mentions the purification of homicides, or the more popular variant that the *Aethiopis* of Arctinus contains the first specific allusion. Every discussion of the subject will be found to start from one or the other of these two dicta.

The assertion that Hesiod alludes to purification in the *Catalogue* is repeated, apparently without verification, in so many of our handbooks, in a tone of such confident dogmatism, that we feel sure the source can be nothing less than the words of an authentic quotation.[10] As a matter of fact, it is simply this: a scholiast to *Iliad*, B. 336, mentions purification in an account of the sack of Pylos by Heracles; when he has finished his story he remarks, "ἱστορεῖ Ἡσίοδος ἐν καταλόγοις," which means no more than "the story is found

[8] For example, Glotz, *Solidarité*, 225 ff.; *Études sur l'antiquité grecque* (Paris, 1906), 27 ff.

[9] Even a hasty inspection will show how constantly discussions of criminal law in the eighth and seventh centuries draw on Aeschylus, Antiphon, Plato, and Demosthenes, and how often they are unable to establish from contemporary sources the presence of the notions with which they are dealing. On the general problem presented by this period, and the sources, cf. *infra* 42.

[10] Naegelsbach, *Homerische Theologie* (Nuremberg, 1884), 267 f.; Schoemann, *Griechische Alterthümer* II (Berlin, 1902), 362; *Recht* 9, n. 25.

in Hesiod's *Catalogue*." The inadequacy of such evidence is pitifully apparent. Even if the scholiast were trying to say that the story as he tells it is taken from Hesiod, it would not justify the assertion that the poet mentions purification, for the mythographers and scholiasts consistently and habitually attribute the customs of their own day to the heroic age.[11]

The other commonplace, that Arctinus in the *Aethiopis* makes the first specific allusion to the purification of homicides,[12] arises from an equally uncritical handling of similar material. Its provenance is a sentence in the prose summary by Proclus, composed probably in the fifth century of the Christian era.[13] Even that sentence has not been considered in its context. Proclus tells us that Achilles slew Thersites because the latter taunted him with his love for Penthesilea. As a result of the slaying, strife befell among the Achaeans, and thereafter Achilles went to Lesbos, where he sacrificed to Apollo, Artemis, and Leto, and was purified of the slaying by Odysseus. Here we have a late writer, who has repeatedly encountered in classical authors the notion that homicide requires lustration, epitomizing in a few words a very considerable portion of the poem, the narrative of a long series of events. What those events were we have but the faintest idea. There was στάσις—strife, dissension—over the killing of Thersites. Was this a simple homicide? Or did Achilles perhaps drag his victim

[11] Cf. Lobeck, *Aglaophamus* (Königsberg, 1829), 969, 300 ff., where a scholiast's comment on *Iliad* xxiv. 480 ff. is taken as an illustration; Thonissen 44, n. 3. A good instance of this tendency is found in two prose arguments to the *Shield*, which speak of purification (Δ. 13 ff.; E. 12 ff.), although the poem itself recognizes in this respect only the ideas of the heroic age (cf. Bonner, *Class. Phil.* VII, 22, and *supra* 26, n. 5).

[12] Glotz, 231; Bréhier, *De Graecorum iudiciorum origine* (Paris, 1899), 76; Bonner, Thonissen, Lipsius, Schoemann, *locc. cit.* Treston (139) must now be added.

[13] It is immaterial whether we ascribe the summary to Proclus the Neoplatonist or to a grammarian of the second or third century A.D.; on the controversy, cf. Sandys, *History of Classical Scholarship* I, 379 f.; Christ, *Geschichte der griechischen Literatur* (ed. 4, 1905), 878 f.

from the altar of the gods to whom he later sacrifices?[14] We do not know. The participation of Odysseus, who is the usual emissary of the host on such occasions, makes the episode, as reported in the summary, look suspiciously like an imitation of the Chryseis story. If the *Iliad* were represented only by an epitome from the pen of Proclus, we might conceivably find in our handbooks the assertion that Homer, in the *Iliad*, specifically alludes to purification for rape. I will cheerfully admit that Arctinus *may* have mentioned the purification of homicide in unequivocal terms, but I think it does not accord with scientific accuracy to base on this flimsy evidence the positive assertion that he *did*; or that this unqualified statement should be handed down, apparently without inspection, from study to study and handbook to handbook, and repeatedly made the starting point for discussion of this important problem.

Thus the somewhat gruesome picture of a society cringing beneath the threat of divine chastisement, completely dominated by the doctrine of pollution, fades under critical inspection, and we see it for what it is—an inference from the literature of later times, unsupported by an authentic citation from a writer earlier than Aeschylus. It goes back to the old assumption, which has already aroused our suspicion, that homicide and its punishment must always be "das Centrum des Criminalrechts." Investigators have been so completely imbued with this feeling that their attention has been focused on homicide to the exclusion of all else. A late scholiast's passing allusion to homicide or purification has been magnified from the tiny molehill it is into a mountain of conjecture, while material of fundamental importance for the history of criminal law has been almost completely ignored, merely because it has nothing to say on the subject of homicide. There is in actual fact not a

[14] Cf. the Cassandra episode in the summary of the *Sack*, where the Greeks wish to stone Ajax for his affront to Athena.

particle of evidence to show that the doctrine of pollution has had any effect upon the administration of justice in this period.[15]

The conception of crime in Hesiod

Hesiod is preeminently the poet of the individual. He sings with keenest zest of the daily life and problems of the peasant household, and the background of his pictures is oftener the tiny rural community than the crowded agora of the growing city-state. His interest in the administration of justice naturally centers in the handling of civil disputes, and some valuable bits of information on this subject are scattered through the *Works and Days*, of which the motif is the poet's unsuccessful litigation with his brother Perses. As in Homeric times, adjudications seem to have been held oftenest in the agora; here the princes who are now the heads of the state sit to decide disputes, and here may always be found a staring throng of interested bystanders.[16] Considerable advance has been made, however, over the practices of the heroic age; witnesses now play a definite part, and their testimony may be given under oath;[17] further-

[15] Vinogradoff apparently misunderstands the preliminary statement of my view published in the *Proceedings of the Classical Association* (XVIII, 87 ff.), and believes that I intend to question the existence of the doctrine in the historical period (*Historical Jurisprudence* II, 185, n. 2). Nothing of course could be farther from my intention, as will appear from a careful reading of the passages in which the subject is discussed. As I have already stated (*supra* 26) the doctrine must have made its appearance as early as the eighth century, although there is no direct evidence for it before Aeschylus. The question of its antiquity is not material to our inquiry, since I think I have shown conclusively that the treatment of homicide exercised no particular influence upon the growth of criminal law, which was chiefly connected with a very different group of facts and ideas (cf. the remainng pages of this chapter and the account of Solon's legislation). The difficult problems involved in the origin and history of the doctrine of pollution offer an inviting field to the student of Greek religious ideas and superstitions; recent studies have made little if any real addition to our knowledge.

[16] *Works*, 28 ff.; cf. *Theog.*, 79–92, 434. It must be remembered that aristocracy has supplanted the Homeric monarchy, and the gerontes, once merely members of the king's council, are now the heads of the state.

[17] *Works*, 282 ff.; cf. 371, 219; Bonner, *Class. Phil.* VII, 18; *Recht*, 11.

more, the aristocracy has apparently devised a compulsory process by which an unwilling opponent may be forced to submit to arbitration.[18]

Since the poet is not inclined to dwell upon the greater problems of public order and well-being unless they have some connection with his more immediate theme, considerable study of his writings will be required to determine whether there has been any marked advance in the definition and punishment of crime.

Though Hesiod says nothing about pollution, and little about homicide,[19] he has intense convictions in regard to right and wrong. He seldom neglects an opportunity to remind us that the gods look with approval upon righteous conduct, and will in the end inevitably punish wickedness. This feeling finds perhaps its best expression in one notable passage in which are enumerated sundry wrongful acts sure to invite divine retribution.[20] Here are found several offenses that the Athenians later included in the category of crime,[21] but it is clear that the poet is looking at them from the standpoint of individual conduct and morality, and has not come to the point of regarding them as crimes. There is, however, one offense that he looks upon as a menace to the whole social order of his day, and that is the perversion of justice. From this he has himself suffered. He does not include it at this point, because it is associated in his mind with the princes who control the state, rather than with the individual citizen, but he comes back to it again and again in the *Works and Days* with a bitter earnestness.

The first allusion to the manipulation of justice by the princes and to their greed for bribes refers specifically to

[18] Bonner, 17–18.

[19] The few scattered allusions to the taking of human life found in the poems can hardly be spoken of as having to do with "homicide."

[20] *Works*, 320–34.

[21] Maltreatment of orphans, abuse of parents, adultery (with a brother's wife).

the poet's own experience with his brother.[22]   As the poem
progresses, however, the reflections upon justice and injustice
assume a more impersonal tone, though Perses is seldom
allowed to forget that the subject is introduced for his
especial edification.   When the folk of the Golden Age are
translated into benevolent daemons, it is their kingly pre-
rogative to watch over the administration of justice and to
punish wrongdoing.[23]   In the account of the succeeding ages
of man, the contrast between lawless violence and orderly
justice is kept constantly before us until we come to the
last and worst epoch, the Age of Iron, in which violence,
wrong, and perjury drive out justice and honor; then do
Shame and Retribution veil their faces and flee from the
abodes of men to take refuge with the gods.[24]   From this
point on, until we come to the maxims and the precepts on
husbandry, the perversion of justice is the all absorbing
theme.   A tumult of indignation is aroused when Justice is
outraged, like a woman dragged wailing through the streets,
by corrupt judges, the authors of "crooked dooms."[25]   With
the evils that await those who drive out justice from their
midst by corrupt judgments, is contrasted the prosperity of
the community where everyone, stranger and citizen alike,
can get a righteous judgment upon his claim and where
transgressions against justice have no place.[26]   The gods are
ever-present among men, and mark well those who oppress
their fellows with "crooked" judgments, in defiance of the
divine will; thrice ten thousand immortal beings, Zeus's
invisible guardians over mortal men, watch over the administration of justice upon the fruitful earth and punish wrongdoing.   The virgin goddess Justice, daughter of Zeus,
revered by the immortals, flees to her father, when men
outrage her with their "crooked" decisions, and complains

[22] 34 ff.

[23] 121 ff.   Some editors regard lines 124–25 as an interpolation from 254–55,
where they are found again; cf. Rzach, *Hesiodi carmina* (Leipzig, 1902), *ad loc.*

[24] 182–201.   [25] 220 ff.   [26] 225–47.

of their injustice; until in time the people requite the arrogant and wicked princes who pervert the course of justice; let the corrupt judges take warning, let them desist from crooked decisions and give righteous judgments.[27] The all-seeing eye of Zeus discerns these conditions, and the god is well aware of the manner in which justice is administered in the state; as things are, the way of the just man is hard, yet the poet is confident that in the end Zeus will not permit injustice to prevail.[28] Zeus has ordained that the lower animals shall live by preying upon one another, but to mankind he has given justice, the noblest of gifts; prosperity will attend upon the man who is just and regards the sanctity of an oath, and upon his house, but the seed of the perjurer is destined to obscurity.[29]

In the *Theogony* the poet is dealing with very different themes, and seldom finds occasion to touch upon political and social conditions, but even here we catch occasional glimpses of the very feeling that underlies the *Works and Days*. There is the picture of the ideal monarch, endowed with wisdom and eloquence, who dispenses justice in righteous dooms, as the folk look on, and by his wise and sure pronouncements quickly terminates even the gravest disputes; so worthily he fulfils the proper function of a king, which is to guide his people aright with wisdom and eloquence if they be misled, that he is revered as a god.[30]   Nereus is termed "The Elder" because he is true and kindly and does not disregard the principles of justice, but has a just and gracious spirit.[31]   In the hateful brood of Eris, after Battles and Murders, come the dissensions of the agora—Disputes and Falsehoods and Wranglings, then the kindred spirits of Lawlessness and insensate Folly, and lastly Horcus, the avenger of perjury.[32]

[27] 249–64.
[28] 267–73. Some modern editors, following the opinion of Plutarch as reported by Proclus, reject these verses as an interpolation; Paley has given a simple and sufficient answer to criticism of the passage (notes *ad loc.*).
[29] 274–85.   [30] *Theog.* 79–92; cf. 434.   [31] 233–36.
[32] 226 ff.; cf. Paley's notes on 228 and 230.

One cannot read far in the *Works and Days* without perceiving that here is the genesis of our political literature. For the first time, an author addresses himself consciously and deliberately to the social and political problems of his day. He presents a vigorous arraignment of things as they are, and also a program of reform, founded upon the two-fold gospel of industry in the individual and justice in those who rule the state. Bitter as is the poet's sense of personal injury, it is almost lost, as he progresses with his theme, in righteous indignation against the greater social wrong of which his own experience is but a single instance. One is tempted, almost, to think that Perses existed only in the poet's mind and the famous lawsuit is but a literary motif employed, with a delicate perfection of art, for an effective approach to the great problem with which the earlier portion of the poem deals.[33]   Of one thing, at any rate, we may be sure; Hesiod viewed the perversion of justice as a crime against society, and not merely a wrong to the individual. Its punishment he leaves to the gods, for he can conceive of no other agency with power and authority to chastise the unjust princes. He is still far from the perfect vision of a state with criminal law and criminal tribunals, but he has anticipated the conception of crime in its fundamental implication.

The lyric poets

Hesiod had found new themes for song, but that song was still the stately hexameter of an earlier age. His successors devised new rhythms for these newer themes, and the domain of epic, become too great and too diverse for a single muse, was broken up among the many lyric modes. Henceforth we must follow our tradition in the remains of

---

[33] Since so extreme nicety of technique would be inconsistent with the patent naiveté of the poem, Croiset is no doubt right in regarding the Perses episode as an actual experience from which the poem grew (*Histoire de la littérature grecque* I [1910], 497).

the lyric poets, which are virtually the only means of first-hand information for the period between Hesiod and Aeschylus. Unfortunately the fragments from this golden age of song are pitifully few, and brief; fortunately they are in most instances the work of great masters, and those great masters are often, like Hesiod, intensely interested in the moral and political problems of their day.

Of the newer forms, none is more like the epic than the elegy and none better fitted for the expression of political ideas. A deliberate and stately measure that yet may be vivacious, uniform but not therefore monotonous, it lends itself alike to philosophic reflection and to earnest propaganda, to brilliant epigram and to reasoned discourse. Above all, it very early became imbued with that personal tone which is inseparable from the discussion of the problems, whether they be moral, social, or political, that touch us closely as individuals. The iambic trimeter has some of these qualities, but not all; it is less adaptable, and was perhaps developed later when elegy already held the field. Hence it is the elegy, and in less degree the iambic, that takes over these among the themes of Hesiod and remains the usual medium for the publication of political ideas until it is in turn displaced by prose. Those political and moral elegies of Tyrtaeus, Solon, and Theognis represented among the extant fragments are alone sufficient to justify the belief that the seventh and sixth centuries possessed a brilliant and vigorous literature of ethical, social, and political discussion, forming a continuous and sustained tradition from Hesiod to the fifth century. In the scant remains of this literature we must seek to trace the concepts with which we are concerned through centuries that saw a doctrine of crime definitely attained and true criminal law produced, centuries that are filled with industrial change and with political and social readjustment.

The ideas to which we have heard Homer allude and
Hesiod devote the impassioned earnestness of his whole soul
are not slow to reappear. As early as Archilochus we find
the familiar juxtaposition of lawless violence and ordered
justice.[34] Tyrtaeus presents the conception of a government
founded upon reciprocal justice and fairness; its members
must be bound by "righteous covenants," all their actions
must be just, and they must not devise ill against the state;
then will victory and might attend upon the people.[35] This
fragment is perhaps from the famous poem "Eunomia," a
political manifesto in the conservative interest, composed
just after the second Messenian war, when economic unrest
threatened a revolution.[36] Here is a significant advance
since Hesiod in the theory of the state, and the conception
of crime is certainly present in the idea of a wrong against
the state.

The political and moral elegy seems to have reached its
highest artistic and creative development, and to have
exerted the greatest influence upon public opinion and political action, in the poetry of Solon. He, like Tyrtaeus, was
a poet-statesman who had helped to bring a long and inde-
cisive war to a successful close, who employed the prestige
he had won to compose political strife and avert civil war.[37]
His watchword also is "Eunomia," but to him the word

[34] Fr. lxxxiv (Hiller-Cr.):

$$\mathring{\omega} \ Z\epsilon\hat{v}, \ \pi\acute{a}\tau\epsilon\rho \ Z\epsilon\hat{v}, \ \sigma\grave{o}\nu \ \mu\grave{\epsilon}\nu \ o\mathring{v}\rho\alpha\nu o\hat{v} \ \kappa\rho\acute{a}\tau os,$$
$$\sigma\grave{v} \ \delta' \ \mathring{\epsilon}\rho\gamma' \ \mathring{\epsilon}\pi' \ \mathring{a}\nu\theta\rho\acute{\omega}\pi\omega\nu \ \acute{o}\rho\hat{q}s$$
$$\lambda\epsilon\omega\rho\gamma\grave{a} \ \kappa\alpha\grave{\iota} \ \theta\epsilon\mu\iota\sigma\tau\acute{a}, \ \sigma o\grave{\iota} \ \delta\grave{\epsilon} \ \theta\eta\rho\acute{\iota}\omega\nu$$
$$\mathring{v}\beta\rho\iota s \ \tau\epsilon \ \kappa\alpha\grave{\iota} \ \delta\acute{\iota}\kappa\eta \ \mu\acute{\epsilon}\lambda\epsilon\iota.$$

(καὶ θεμιστά, σοὶ: Liebel for κάθέμιστας, οἱ)

[35] Fr. ii (Hiller-Cr.). These few lines present the essential outlines of the
Spartan polity tersely and clearly.

[36] Ar. Pol. 1306 b 39 ff. Cf. the critical notes of Crusius (Anth. Lyr. xv).
Eduard Meyer's argument against the view that this is a quotation from "Eunomia" is not convincing (Forschungen zur alten Geschichte I, 227 ff.). It is a mistake
to give to δήμου πλήθει the technical meaning it might have had in the partisan
literature of the late fifth century.

[37] Cf. Linforth, 39 ff., 53 ff.

stands for a new order, and not a blind adherence to the old.[38] Probably no single fact which has come down to us from this obscure period throws more light upon the political and social ideas at work in the Greek cities than this, that conservative and progressive alike made "Eunomia" their slogan.   The notion that the state cannot prosper without justice and good order, faintly foreshadowed in Homer and passionately proclaimed by Hesiod, has become the mainspring of political activity.   Men are now aware that they need not put their trust solely in a divine justice; they know that a remedy lies within the state, and in this quest they seek to modify constitutions and to promulgate written codes.   "Eunomia"—the Reign of Law, that justice and order without which society cannot prosper—is the rallying cry in the bitter struggles of the seventh and sixth centuries, the goal—ostensibly, at least—of every concerted movement toward political ends, whether its tendency be progressive or conservative.

   If this be true, if in these centuries the responsibility of the state for the security and well-being of its individual members is coming to be recognized, if justice and good order are the prevailing theme of political thought and discussion, we may reasonably expect to find that tremendous strides have been made in political thought, and particularly in the development of a conception of crime, since the time of Hesiod.   There is among the survivals from Solon's poetry a passage which would alone suffice to answer our question, even if there were not another line from this period.   It is

[38] *Ibid.*, 66 ff.   A most interesting and instructive comparison might be drawn between the "liberal conservatism"—if we may use an expression so abused—of Solon and the unreasoning adherence of Theognis to the old order (cf. *infra* 40 f.). Solon unquestionably desired to restore and maintain the former political condition of Attica, but with remarkable acumen he perceived that this could be done only—if at all—by accommodating the laws and the machinery for their administration to the altered conditions of economic and social life.   He was far more intelligent than the average conservative of his time, or, unfortunately, our own. For brief comments on the general character of his political achievements, cf. *infra* 88.

the famous elegy quoted by Demosthenes against Aeschines,[39] which begins:

'Ημετέρη δὲ πόλις κατὰ μὲν Διὸς οὔποτ' ὀλεῖται
αἶσαν καὶ μακάρων θεῶν φρένας ἀθανάτων.

Here Solon enumerates the manifold evils which threaten disaster to the state, and proposes a remedy. The ruin which impends, he tells us, will come, not by the will of the blessed gods, but from the greed and folly of the citizens and from the unjust spirit of their leaders, whose lawless outrages will be punished by many woes; they are not content to hold their insolence in check and enjoy the blessings they have, but grow rich on injustice and pillage alike the sacred and the public treasures; "they pay no heed to the unshaken rock of holy Justice."[40] These crimes have now spread like a festering sore over the whole state, which has fallen into shameful servitude, the cause of internecine strife, and is wasted by the secret conspiracies of unjust men; no one is safe even in his home from this public evil. Lawlessness is the chief source of evil to the state; the remedy is to be found in the Reign of Law, Eunomia, which brings order and harmony, fetters evildoers, does away with insolent and lawless outrage, corrects "crooked" judgments, puts an end to arrogance and sedition and angry strife, and brings to mankind moderation and wisdom.

From the very start the poet makes us feel that he is not speaking of private wrongs or sins, to be punished by the individual victim, or left to divine retribution. He tells us with insistent repetition that these are crimes; they menace the state with disaster; they spread over the whole state like a festering sore that cannot be checked; they constitute a public evil from which the individual citizen cannot escape unaided.[41] The only remedy is the Reign of Law, which will

[39] Dem. xix. 255 (Hiller-Cr. fr. ii).
[40] Linforth's translation (p. 141; cf. note ad loc.).
[41] Lines 5 ff., 17 ff., 27 ff.

shackle criminals and repress their crimes.[42] The recognition of the nature and consequences of crime which underlies
the imaginative and poetic diction is so complete, the formulation of basic principles on which crime is to be dealt with
so distinct, that one might search far in modern political
writings without finding these ideas more adequately treated
in so few words.   It is no mere coincidence that the author
is that man whom tradition honored as the first to establish
permanent machinery for the punishment of crimes by the
state.   Nor is it entirely without significance that the specific
evils chosen by Solon to illustrate his conception—theft of
sacred or of public moneys, the perversion of justice, sedition
and civil strife, conspiracy against the common weal, the
enslavement of poor citizens[43]—seem very early to have been
the subject of stringent criminal legislation in Athens, or
that the two crimes which he selects for repetition in the
closing lines were already in Homeric times coming to be
looked upon as offenses against society.[44] We have here a
thread of tradition that runs through centuries.   The political consciousness which was beginning faintly to awake in
the Homeric age has now formulated the conception of crime,
and the time is ripe for application of the principle that has
been evolved.

   With the poets who follow Solon, political elegy has
passed beyond the great creative age.   But it is still the
principal if not the only medium for the general diffusion of
reflections upon social and political problems, and the opportunity it affords to pursue further the development of these
ideas must not be neglected.   The step which Solon took
when he enacted true criminal legislation, founded upon a
doctrine of crime adequate to the needs of society, was one
of fundamental importance; it was, as we shall see when we
come to analyze it, one of the greatest strides the human

[42] Lines 32 ff.   [43] Lines 12–25.
[44] Lines 36–37 (perversion of justice and civil strife; cf. *supra* 22).

mind has ever taken in the realm of politics and jurisprudence. But even so it was but the first step in a rather
long phase of legal development, and we must study the
ideas which were current during that development as well as
those which prompted the first step. A very considerable
body of elegiac verse attributed to Theognis of Megara may
fairly be taken to represent the trend of thought in Hellas
during the latter part of the sixth century.[45]

In a series of verses addressed to Cyrnus, Theognis
describes as he sees them the evils which threaten the state
with disaster.[46] The state is pregnant, and the poet fears a
tyrant will be born to correct her lawlessness. The citizens
are not responsible for this, but rather their lowborn leaders;
when the base take pleasure in lawless outrage, when they
despoil the people and give judgments in the interest of
dishonest men with an eye to their own profit and power,
when they delight in gains derived from the injury of the
state, then hope not that the state can escape calamity,
whatever may be its apparent security. From such crimes
are bred seditions and civil wars and tyrannies. Here we
have in somewhat different language Solon's list of crimes
and the same firm conviction that they involve disaster to
the whole state and not merely to individuals. Theognis,
however, is a keen partisan, and his poems are party mani-
festoes, though none the less instructive if we wish to study
the thought of his time. How different is his viewpoint
from that of Solon is seen in the lines in which he attributes
these evils to the ascendancy of men who once, he tells us

[45] Fortunately we are not concerned with the numerous doubts that have
been raised as to the Theognidean authorship of specific lines; the ideas with
which we have to do are discussed in the earlier part of the collection, which is
unanimously regarded as the work of Theognis, and bears the hall-mark of the
author—the address to Cyrnus. In general, the verses of the first book may be
regarded as coming from the poet's time if not, in every instance, actually from
his pen; we may note the difference between the intense personal note of the
passages to which I refer and the proverbial distichs and quatrains that pre-
dominate in the latter part of the collection.

[46] Lines 39–52, 53–68 (Hiller-Cr.).

bitterly, lived without the city in wretched poverty, knowing
naught of law or justice; they now are exalted and the former
leaders are abased.[47] His remedy seems to be the exact
reverse of Solon's for he would trust in the gods and hope
for a return to the old and better order; but we more than
suspect that his rallying cry is the old familiar watchword
"Eunomia," Good Government.[48]

The fragments which have yielded this comparatively
rich array of ideas regarding good order in the state and the
problems of crime, have nothing whatsoever to say in regard
to homicide or pollution and purification.   This brief survey
seems to me to show rather clearly that criminal law in
ancient Hellas was evolved quite independently of any
influence that may be attributed particularly to the ideas
regarding homicide or pollution; it was not in any sense a
by-product of superstitious ceremonial, but resulted rather
from the development and conscious application of a rational
doctrine of crime.   This opinion may now be further tested
by examining in detail Solon's enactment of criminal law
and the problems for which it was intended to provide a
solution.

[47] Lines 53 ff.

[48] Cf. the allusion to "eunomia" in Xenophanes (*fr.* ii. 19 [Hiller-Cr.]), where
the predominant interest seems to be economic.

CHAPTER IV

THE ENACTMENT OF TRUE CRIMINAL LAW
IN ATHENS

Since the texts discussed in the preceding chapter are but scattered fragments, infinitesimal in comparison with what has been lost, it would be quite unreasonable to deny the presence of any idea, or disregard its possible influence, simply because no allusion to it is preserved. But after all these are our only authentic sources of information for the eighth and seventh centuries. Furthermore they are specimens, chosen for a variety of purposes by different writers from diverse sources, but by the natural processes of selection largely from the best and most important, and through them only can we hope to know the spirit and temper of the age. When we undertake to discover what doctrines are most likely to have influenced political and social thought during this critical period in the history of Western institutions, and what problems chiefly occupied men's minds, our main reliance must be these fragments, and not fanciful conceptions of what men *may* have thought. Nothing could justify us in passing over ideas that bulk large in these quotations from the great poets and thinkers of the day and substituting notions gleaned from the writings of a later age. We are forced to the conclusion that the Hellenes of the eighth and seventh centuries gave little or no thought to the criminal aspects of simple homicide; their attention was directed mainly to the greater offenses that immediately and patently menaced the common welfare and to the possibility of effective repression. If we may once more pin our faith to the extant sources, this interest in the problems of crime and its punishment by the body politic found its most complete and vigorous expression in Attica toward the end of the seventh century, in the political poems of Solon.

We have observed that criminal law emerges from the primitive law of tort when the right of action arising from a wrong, or delict, ceases to be restricted to the immediate victim, and is granted, in the case of certain offenses, to any citizen who may care to exercise it—that is to say, vested in the body politic. There is no reason to question the statement of Aristotle that in Athens it was Solon who took this important step,[1] or to reject Plutarch's opinion that it was intended to protect the lower classes in their weakness against the aggression of the rich and powerful.[2] We cannot think of anyone who is more likely to have been the author of this innovation than Solon, or better qualified to see to its enactment, if we may judge by what we know of him from his own writings; nor would it be easy to suggest a more favorable opportunity for such a change than was presented by Solon's appointment as special nomothete with dictatorial powers.[3] It is now in order to consider attentively the political and economic conditions that prompted this appointment, so far as they may be determined, and the more pressing problems which confronted the legislator. We shall then perhaps be able to appraise somewhat more definitely the place of the provision in Solon's program and to throw some light upon the precise form of its enactment.

The condition of
Attica before Solon

The attempt to describe the social, political, and economic conditions which prevailed in Attica before the archonship of Solon must begin with a frank confession that we know very

---

[1] *Cons. Ath.* ix. 1.   [2] *Solon* xviii. *fin.*

[3] Ar. *Cons. Ath.* v, vi. 1.   The extent of Solon's powers is clearly shown in the language he himself uses of his reforms, especially in *fr.* xxxii. 15–25 (Hiller-Cr.). Cf. Linforth 46, 59.

little of details.   But a number of important facts are definitely established, and the main outlines of the picture may be traced with some assurance.[4]   All functions of government, legislative, executive, and judicial, in so far as they have developed, have long been exclusively in the hands of the eupatrid class, which acts through the aristocratic council later known as the Council of the Areopagus[5] and executive officers of its choosing.[6]   Within this ruling class the basis of preferment appears to be partly aristocratic and partly timocratic.[7]   The inferior orders of citizens, the peasant proprietors, or georgi, and the artisans, the demiurgi, apparently cannot hope to have any part in the government except by attaching themselves to some member of the aristocracy.[8] Below the georgi and demiurgi are the lowest class of freemen, the propertyless population, variously termed thetes, hectemori, pelatae, who seem to have fewer rights, if that be possible, and in many cases to be virtually serfs.[9]   Still lower are the slaves, mere chattels without rights of any kind.

When we undertake to define more precisely the rights enjoyed by the georgi and demiurgi and to formulate the distinction between these inferior orders of citizens and the free inhabitants of Attica who are not citizens, we at once become aware that the statements in our histories are extremely vague and unsatisfactory.   There is much talk of

[4] Ar. *Cons. Ath.* ii–iii.   Cf. Busolt II (1895), 90–247, especially 93–98, 106–24, 136–95, 243–47; Linforth, 28–32, 47–52; Meyer, *Geschichte des Alterthums* II (Stuttgart, 1893), 291–361, 636 ff.

[5] Ar. *Cons. Ath.* iii. 6.

[6] *Ibid.* viii. 2.   This definite statement cannot be ignored because of the apparent contradictions in *Pol.* 1273 b 39 ff.   On the other hand, cf. Busolt II, 143, n. 2.

[7] *Ibid.* iii. 1.

[8] *Ibid.* ii. 3: οὐδενὸς γὰρ ὡς εἰπεῖν ἐτύγχανον μετέχοντες.   In this chapter Aristotle clearly is thinking of the whole δῆμος, not merely of the non-citizens, though he lays particular stress upon the sad plight of the ἐκτήμοροι.   On the condition of the peasant under the aristocracy, cf. Meyer II, 305 ff., 642 ff.

[9] Ar. *Cons. Ath.* ii. 2 (πελάται καὶ ἐκτήμοροι); vii. 3 (θῆτες).   Much attention has been given to the discrimination of these terms (cf. Meyer II, 642–43, 652 ff.; Gilbert, *Constitutional Antiquities of Sparta and Athens* [London, 1893], 117 f.; Busolt II, 108 ff., and the studies there cited).   We need note only that they refer to the lower classes of freemen, who are clearly not part of the body politic.

"citizens" and "non-citizens," of those who possess "das Bürgerrecht" and of the "nichtbürgerliche Athener" but no attempt to say definitely in what "citizenship" consists.[10] We are sometimes told, it is true, that citizens were privileged to attend the assembly, but the functions and powers of the assembly are not defined.[11] A good example of this uncertainty of thought is Bury's remark[12] that, in the period just before Solon's reform, "The Thetes were citizens, but had no political rights." If I may be permitted to suggest in very general terms a method of approach which may possibly lead to a better understanding, it is this. The state is still organized, as in Homeric times, on a basis of families and phratries, not of individuals. Its government is actually carried on by the aristocratic council, in which the phratries, and no doubt all families of great wealth and influence, are represented;[13] conversely, the body politic is the collective membership of these families and phratries. That is to say, the individual whose connection, be it actual or fictitious, with one of the kinship groups represented in the council is recognized, is a member of a phratry and a citizen. It was entirely natural in a simple condition of society that this recognition should extend to respectable peasant farmers and artisans. They were landowners on a

[10] If we accept the "Draconian constitution," we can ascribe definite rights to the inferior orders of citizens, e.g., membership in the council (Ar. *Cons. Ath.* iv. 3). However, aside from other objections that may be urged, I find it quite impossible to reconcile the account of the "Draconian constitution" with what we know of the early history of Attica and of the evolution of government in other states; it is apparently drawn, not from history, but from reconstructions by political doctrinaires. (For discussions of this subject, cf. Sandys's notes; De Sanctis, 159–66; Busolt II, 36 f., 224, n. 3, and the studies these authors cite). If the "Draconian constitution" be rejected—and few historians now accept it—it is very difficult to say in what precise respects the inferior orders of citizens were distinguished from the free, non-burgess population (cf. Busolt II, 108–10; Meyer II, 305–6).

[11] Bury, *History of Greece to the Death of Alexander* (London, 1904), 174. The view (173) that the assembly elected the magistrates, or nominated candidates from whose number the council made a selection, is open to suspicion on the score of what little we know of the political institutions of this period and directly contradicts the statement of Aristotle (*Cons. Ath.* viii. 2) on the subject. On the assembly under the aristocracy, cf. Meyer II, 334.

[12] 176. [13] I am of course not speaking of representation in the technical sense.

small scale, and were able to maintain their membership in the phratries because they could pay their "scot" when meetings and festivals came around. They were the folk who were mustered by phratries and tribes for military service, and attended the assembly. It was likewise inevitable that the propertyless classes, the hectemori and hired laborers, should be excluded from the phratries and consequently from citizenship.[14]

[14] This analysis of the early aristocratic organization of the state in Attica involves some departures from the prevailing opinion, which appears to assume the existence, as early as the Homeric age, of two distinct elements in the state, (1) the "noble" families, organized as clans (γένη) for the worship of divine ancestors, who constitute the original membership of the phratries and phylae, and (2) the "commons," not connected with the nobility by bonds of kinship, who gradually force their way into the phylae and phratries and finally organize themselves into groups patterned after the clans. I am inclined to think that this theory requires some modification. It proceeds in part from modern preconceptions touching nobility of birth, and from the temptation to transfer to Athens the Roman division into patricians and plebeians, to which the analogy between "patrician" and the Greek εὐπατρίδης invites. If it be subjected to critical examination, it will be found to rest chiefly on assumptions, rather than on facts which may be verified from the sources. In the *Iliad* what is almost the sole allusion to the phratries and tribes shows clearly that they included the mass of the folk and not a ruling nobility only (ii. 362–66; however, for arguments against the authenticity of this passage, cf. Leaf, *Homer and History*, 260 f.). We get our clearest picture of a Homeric community in the *Odyssey*, and here again we can scarcely doubt that the little groups comprising the free population of Ithaca are kinship groups in which the free members, leaders and followers alike, are blood-relations (cf. especially *Odyssey* xxiv. 412 ff.). The leaders of these groups are Zeus-born kings, who regard the house of Odysseus merely as first among its peers (cf. *Odyssey* i. 389–98). What we know of the earliest condition of Attica accords with this, and it is reasonable to believe that the Eupatrids are the leaders of the local groups, the immediate connections of the chieftains who from petty kings (βασιλεῖς) become, first, members of the king's council and later the rulers of the aristocratic state. Their primacy is not so much the result of a difference of descent or race as a development within the kinship group. With the increased wealth and power that attend upon this primacy (cf. *Odyssey* i. 390–93), and the increasing importance of horizontal divisions engendered by the process of aggregation, they tend more and more to become a class, distinct from the mass of the folk. The old relationships with the commons may have been ignored in the clans, but were no doubt religiously recognized in the phratries. The view that I have briefly outlined agrees in some particulars with that developed by Meyer in the second volume of his *Geschichte des Alterthums*, and adopted by De Sanctis (56 ff.), though I should put the effective development of a "noble" class later than the Homeric age. Cf. Busolt II, 113 ff. for the citation of important studies. Grote, writing more than half a century ago, came much nearer to a satisfactory analysis of this difficult problem than many of his successors. "The Eupatridae are the wealthy and powerful men, belonging to the most distinguished families in all the various gentes, and principally living in the city of Athens, after the consolidation of Attica: from them are distinguished the middling and lower people, roughly classified into husbandmen and artisans." (*History of Greece* III, 97.)

I am inclined to think that historians overestimate the importance of the assembly under the aristocracy; it has added little if anything to the functions and powers of the Homeric assembly.[15] Probably it exercises no direct influence upon the conduct of government except in so far as the council may hesitate to disregard entirely a vigorous and decided expression of popular opinion. Such rights as the inferior orders of citizens enjoy are assured to them rather by virtue of their membership in the phratries and their connection with aristocratic families whose heads are members of the council. The meaner citizens, the distant connections of aristocratic families, are probably obliged to cultivate the good will of their more influential relatives, who are members of the inner circle, if they wish to derive any real advantage from their inclusion in the body politic, and the relation of the head of a family to its poorer members must be, in effect, somewhat like that between the Roman patron and his clients.[16] It is of course probable that aliens resident in Attica may enter into a somewhat similar relationship toward influential citizens and thereby secure a measure of protection and even of privilege, especially if they are men of wealth; but we can scarcely doubt, in the light of what we know regarding the treatment of aliens in later times,[17] that the citizen, by reason of his connection with a group that is directly represented in the government, is at a great advantage as compared with an alien of the same wealth and social standing. In addition to this it is likely that the laws and custom upon which the individual depends for the security of his person and property set up distinctions between citizens and non-citizens comparable to the discrimination in the Cretan law of the fifth century

[15] *Supra* 45, n. 11.

[16] Cf. Meyer II, 305, 332.

[17] Cf. Clerq, *Les métèques athéniens* (Paris, 1893); Gilbert, 176 ff.; on the rights of metics in the courts, cf. *infra* 53.

between members of hetaeries (ἐλεύθεροι) and non-members (ἀπέταιροι).[18]

What we have here is an organization of society by families and kinship, interpenetrated, or "shot across," with graduations based upon occupation and economic status. The beginnings of this graduation can be seen within the patriarchal family, and we find traces of it in the poems of Homer, but it is still relatively unimportant in comparison with the system founded upon actual or fictitious kinship.[19] In the process of aggregation into ever larger social groups, these horizontal strata naturally play an increasing part in social and political life, and "class consciousness" tends to supersede the spiritual unity of family and clan. In Attica in the period under discussion these changes were undoubtedly accelerated by the rapid expansion of commerce and industry. There is some reason to believe that by Solon's time the center of gravity had so shifted that political privilege was proportionate to economic status, with certain restrictions to be discussed; probably the distribution of the citizens into the four property classes that are the basis of the Solonian constitution was already recognized for some purposes of government.[20]

Effects of
economic changes

The reader will perhaps expect the tendencies that have been sketched to bring about a simple, direct progression toward a constitution in which the timocratic principle will replace the aristocratic. But this process of substitution

[18] Cf. *Recueil* I, 418 ff.; on the status of metics at this time in Attica, cf. Clerq, 331 f.

[19] Seymour, 291 ff.; Fanta, *Der Staat in der Ilias und Odyssee* (Innsbruck, 1882), cites a number of passages which show the beginnings of an occupational classification (43 ff.).

[20] Cf. Linforth 77; De Sanctis 229–31; Busolt II, 180 ff. No doubt these classes had long been recognized in the allocation of duties and burdens by the state, and Solon first made them a basis for the graduation of political privilege.

was retarded and interrupted at every step by the inherent conviction, apparently an ancient and common heritage of the Hellenes, that the primary criterion of citizenship must be descent.   Had the Athenian aristocracy held fast to this single principle, the course of events would have resolved itself into a struggle between a growing industrial and commercial population, largely alien, and the agricultural folk, chiefly indigenous, who would have opposed to any invasion of their prerogatives a united resistance, except perhaps for some disaffection on the part of the lower orders.   But the aristocracy, as was to be expected, did not hold fast, and its partial surrender, in conjunction with economic influences, complicated the struggle and hastened the catastrophe. The partial surrender was this, a property qualification was made a prerequisite of citizenship, but not the sole prerequisite; to be entitled to membership in the body politic a man must combine with the proper financial status a hereditary right.[21]

The actual workings of this twofold standard were determined by the general trend of economic conditions and by the usages of the time with regard to money and credit. Attica, like many other parts of Greece, was unable to support a large population on the products of her soil.[22]

[21] It is inherently unlikely that a definite census was explicitly set as a prerequisite to citizenship, in these early times.   But it was natural, in fact inevitable (cf. *supra* 45 f.) that citizens who lost their land and sank to the position of hectemori should not long retain their connection with more prosperous kinsmen or with the phratries.   In fact, unless this took place, we cannot understand Solon's account of the conditions he found, or the measures by which he tells us he undertook to set them aright (*infra* 54).   The other factor in this twofold standard, the insistence on hereditary right, persisted for centuries, and was abandoned only temporarily at times of grave peril (e.g., in the archonship of Clisthenes, at the time of the battle of Arginusae, etc.), though grants of citizenship to individuals gradually came to be made rather freely.   The effects of rigorous insistence on the twofold standard are abundantly exemplified in the later history of Sparta.

[22] Thuc. I. ii. 5.   Cf. Meyer II, 637; Curtius, *Stadtgeschichte von Athen* (Berlin, 1891), 12 ; Neumann-Partsch, *Physikalische Geographie von Griechenland* (Breslau, 1885), 347 f., 354 f.   The dependence of Athens on importation of grain is perhaps foreshadowed by the aggressive movements in the Pontic region as early as the end of the seventh century (cf. Busolt II, 249 ff.); on the scarcity of wheat in early times, cf. Neumann-Partsch, 445.   Gilliard (139 ff.) thinks that in these

But her mineral wealth, especially her potter's clay, combined with a situation favorable for manufacture and export, tended to attract immigration.[23]   As a result, at a time when other communities were providing for their excess population by colonization and emigration, Athens seems to have been steadily adding to a population which it is likely already taxed her natural resources.[24]   The immigrants were no doubt supported to some extent by importation of foodstuffs, for which they paid with the returns from their industrial and commercial enterprises.   This situation was favorable to the large landowner who produced in quantity and was glad of a market for his surplus commodities.   But it was very difficult for the peasant farmer whose little plot of none too fertile ground would just maintain his family in a normal year.   When a poor season came, he had to turn to his

times Attica could even afford to export grain.   But the attempt to prove this by computing the surplus production of the pentacosiomedimnus fails, when we find that one factor, essential in any valid computation, is absolutely an unknown quantity—the number of pentacosiomedimni; for all we know, they may have been very few indeed in this period.   Nor can we found an opinion (Busolt II, 247, n. 4) on the law attributed to Solon forbidding exportation of grain (Plut. *Solon* xxiv); the prosperous commercial neighbors of Athens may well have offered tempting markets at times when the poorer folk of Attica were starving; in fact one may just as well cite the embargo to prove that Attica did not produce sufficient grain for her population (De Sanctis, 193, n. 3).   Gilliard's theory (141 f.) that the law is not an economic measure but a very ancient military ordinance by which grain was looked on as "contraband of war" seems to me quite fanciful.

[23] Neumann-Partsch, 271; silver was mined, though not extensively, from very early times (Ardaillon, *Les mines du Laurion dans l'antiquité* [Paris, 1897], 126 ff.).

[24] That Athens did not participate in the great colonizing movements of the eighth and seventh centuries is of course well known.   But historians pass over virtually without a word the possibilities of early immigration into Attica, with its bearings upon the economic and political situation.   Yet there must have been considerable immigration even as early as the seventh century.   It is reflected in the various foreign influences successively exhibited in Attic pottery, and particularly in the change from earlier customs of dress and burial to the wearing of the Ionic chiton and the practice of burning the dead, innovations which belong to the seventh century.   (Cf. Busolt II, 199 f.)   Furthermore, it is a priori unlikely that a state so situated as Athens could have remained unaffected by the continual migration of this period; only isolated communities are likely to be untouched by such movements.   If Attica was not sending out emigrants, when the whole Hellenic world was on the move, she was likely receiving settlers from other localities.   Clerq, who has studied the subject carefully, believes there was a considerable alien population resident in Attica from very early times (327 ff., especially 329).

wealthy neighbor; since the use of money had replaced the practice of barter,[25] he could not borrow commodities, to be repaid in kind, but only money, on the security of his farm or even the persons of himself and his family;[26] with this money he must buy in a market where prices were affected by the demands of a prosperous commercial population. When he bought, prices were high; when he had surplus produce to sell, presumably they would be lower. The result is easily foreseen. Mortgages were constantly being foreclosed;[27] the persons of debtors and their families were being seized. The agricultural regions of Attica were passing into the hands of a comparatively few enormously wealthy men, and the peasant class was rapidly dwindling, as its members were reduced to the condition of hired workers or even to slavery.[28] The general distress was made more acute by a long-continued war with Megara.[29] Though we hear nothing regarding the free native demiurgi, we may well believe that they were suffering in equal measure from the competition of larger and more efficient industrial establishments, which no doubt employed slave labor and were at a great advantage alike in procuring raw materials and in disposing of their products. Many of the demiurgi, like the georgi, must have lost their citizen status and become hired laborers or slaves.[30]

If this analysis be sound, we can easily understand the causes of Solon's appointment as special nomothete and the

[25] Cf. Meyer II, 549 ff.

[26] Ar. *Cons. Ath.* ii. 2; iv. 5; cf. Linforth, 50 f.

[27] We are not concerned here with the controversy regarding the precise nature of the transaction; it is immaterial to our inquiry whether the creditor foreclosed upon the actual land, or upon the major portion of its products, or upon the person. By any of these theories, the georgus who is unable to repay a loan becomes a hectemorus, and the hectemorus who cannot meet his obligations to his lord is made a chattel slave, along with the members of his family. Starting from the economic situation that has been outlined, by any of these paths we come inevitably to the social and political conditions described by Solon and Aristotle. Cf. Linforth, 62 f.; Gilliard, 124 ff., especially 128 f., and, for the controversial studies of the subject, De Sanctis, 194 ff.

[28] Solon *fr.* xxxii (Hiller-Cr.); cf. Busolt II, 243 ff.; Gilliard, 144 ff.

[29] Cf. Busolt II, 247.   [30] Cf. Gilliard, 138.

nature of the problems that confronted him.   In fact, much of what we have been able to infer from the general economic situation is set forth explicitly in the fragments of his poems.[31] The burgess body has been greatly reduced, and is in effect the membership of the wealthy families who now possess nearly all the agricultural land of Attica.   Many peasant farmers and artisans, once citizens, have been degraded to the position of landless hirelings, whose lot it is to toil under wealthy lords for a meager share of what they produce; others have actually been reduced to slavery with their families, or have sold their children as slaves, and many of these unhappy chattels have been sold into other lands; still others have themselves fled from Attica as the only way of escaping the fate to which a burden of debt exposes them. To put it briefly, we have an oligarchy of the wealthy and privileged ruling over a large proletariat, which is kept in utter subjection politically and unremittingly made the object of merciless economic exploitation.   The bulk of the native middle class apparently has been distributed between the two extremes.   In such a situation the alternative to revolution and perhaps tyranny was compromise,[32] and this the ruling class, or some of them, were wise enough to see. And we must believe that these wiser men were keenly alive to the menace which confronted them in the presence of a prosperous alien population, chafing under the denial of the political rights to which their economic strength entitled them, ready at the first opportunity to fan into the flame of revolution the smouldering discontent of the native proletariat.[33]

The administration of justice was part and parcel of this political and economic system.   Offenses against the state, and probably wrongs of an exceptionally flagrant character, could be carried directly to the aristocratic council by persons

[31] Especially *frs.* xxxii, ii, vii, ix (Hiller-Cr.).

[32] *Fr.* ii. 17–20; cf. *frs.* vii, ix (Hiller-Cr.).   Cf. Linforth, 57.   [33] *Supra* 50.

of some influence or power.[34] Transgressions of individual rights were dealt with in accordance with the primitive law of tort, and could be brought to the attention of the aristocratic magistrates, the executive officers of the council, whose decisions were final;[35] the right of action was restricted to the injured individual. It would be quite unreasonable to assume that in this age non-citizens enjoyed legal rights which were denied to them in the fifth and fourth centuries.[36] Therefore it is certain that only burgesses could sue in the courts; all others, irrespective of wealth, must have been dependent upon the good offices of citizens to whom they might attach themselves as clients. Under such a system it is clear that only citizens, and probably only influential citizens, could count upon any real protection from the law, and we are not surprised to find the perversion of justice among the evils which especially arouse Solon's indignation.[37]

Solon's program of reform

We have fortunately had before us in the fragments Solon's authentic statement of these conditions and the way in which he proposes to deal with them.[38] (The blind greed and dishonesty of those who rule the state, and the specific abuses that are the consequence, threaten utter ruin;[39] Solon proposes to terminate these evils and avert the catas-

[34] Infra 82.

[35] Ar. Cons. Ath. iii. 5. Cf. Linforth, 51 f.; De Sanctis, 197. The administration of justice before Solon has recently been made the subject of a careful, detailed investigation (Gertrude Smith, The Administration of Justice from Hesiod to Solon [Chicago Dissertation, 1924]).

[36] Cf. Lipsius, Recht, 791 f.; Gilbert, 182. Even in the fourth century, apparently, only especially privileged metics, perhaps only proxeni, could sue in the court of the polemarch in propria persona. Clerq (260 ff.) believes that metics required no intermediary before the courts; even if we accept this view, however, we cannot well account for the existence of the prostate in the fourth century, which Clerq admits (265), except on the assumption that in earlier times he was a genuine representative of the metic in all transactions with the state, including those in the courts.

[37] Supra 39.   [38] Supra 38 f.   [39] Fr. ii (Hiller-Cr.).

trophe by instituting the "Reign of Law" and founding the
state on ordered justice.[40] But he means justice in the very
broadest sense, as his own words show, and the fundamental
adjustments with which he began were mainly economic.
As he says in his later poems, he freed Mother Earth from
her bondage and removed the tablets of stone that were the
marks of her servitude. This is generally understood to be
an allusion to the famous "Seisachtheia," or cancellation of
debts, which must have affected all obligations contracted
on the security of land or the person of the debtor.[41] He
brought home the Athenians who had been sold as slaves in
foreign lands or had fled from Attica to escape the fate their
load of debt made inevitable, and restored to liberty those
who were living as slaves at home.[42] These were the
measures by which he endeavored to restore the victims of
economic pressure to their original status and to heal the
diseased condition of the body politic. They were retro-
active in their effect, and are properly described by Linforth
as "temporary expedients," intended to meet immediate
exigencies and distinct from the "permanent regulations"
which looked to the future.[43] If Solon made any attempt
to deal with the underlying economic forces, it cannot have
gone much further than the changes in weights, measures,
and currency which tradition ascribes to him[44] and possibly
an embargo on the exportation of certain staples.[45] It is
certain that he did not proceed to a redistribution of the
land and did nothing to alleviate the oppressive burdens of
the hectemori.[46] Consequently when the beneficiaries of
these temporary expedients had been restored to their former

[40] Fr. ii. lines 32 ff.

[41] Fr. xxxii. 5 ff. (Hiller-Cr.); Ar. Cons. Ath. xii. 4. Cf. Linforth, 62 ff.;
Gilliard, 188 ff.; De Sanctis, 206 ff.; Busolt II, 259, n. 2 fin.

[42] Ibid. lines 8 ff.

[43] 62.

[44] Ar. Cons. Ath. x. Cf. Linforth, 287 ff., with the studies cited.

[45] Supra 49, n. 22.

[46] Frs. iii, iv, xxx-xxxii b (Hiller-Cr.). Cf. Busolt II, 261 f.

status, they must have found themselves so abjectly weak, individually and collectively, politically and economically, as to be completely at the mercy of the powerful aristocracy. It was a foregone conclusion that, unless something should be done for their protection, they would speedily succumb again to the forces which had caused their former misfortunes and fall once more into the degradation from which Solon had raised them. It was incumbent on the nomothete to provide this protection if his work was to endure. Since he had declined to confer upon the proletariat that measure of economic strength which would enable them to maintain their position against the aggression of the upper classes, it was left for him to meet this necessity, so far as possible, by his laws and judicial reforms. This must have been the first and greatest of his problems.[47] And it is here that we may hope to discern more precisely the motives that prompted his introduction of the public action.

(One of the measures, and probably the most important, by which Solon attempted to prevent the degradation of citizens we know. It prohibited the seizure of the person for debt.[48] Another, which may be pronounced authentic with but little hesitation, since it is a necessary complement of the first, prohibited the sale of a child by a parent or of a sister by a brother.[49] Solon no doubt took cognizance of other acts by which citizens might be deprived of their rights or degraded to slavery, but we can be certain only of the two laws mentioned. Something more was needed, however, than the mere enactment of such laws; whatever their number and the severity of the penalties provided, they could not have the desired effect if they should be administered by the aristocracy, as of old, through magistrates invested with

[47] To this he recurs first and most earnestly in his account of his reforms (fr. xxxii [Hiller-Cr.]).

[48] Ar. Cons. Ath. vi. 1; ix. 1; Plut. Solon xv; Diog. Laert. i. 45. Cf. Linforth, 72; Gilliard, 175 ff.; infra 78 f.

[49] Plut. Solon xxiii. Cf. Gilliard, 177, n. 2.

the right of final judgment. In order to make his enactments a real safeguard against a recurrence of the conditions he had sought to terminate, the nomothete established popular courts and provided for an appeal from the decisions of the aristocratic magistrates.[50] But even this, though it is justly called the cornerstone of Athenian democracy, was not enough. (The body politic must exercise not only the right of final judgment, but also the right of initiating prosecutions; if the laws intended to protect the weaker citizens were to function properly every step in the process of their administration must be subjected to popular control.) The individual must not be left dependent on his unaided efforts to procure the intervention of the law, he must be able to rely on the support of his fellow-citizens. Here the primitive law of tort, by which the individual was the sole avenger of his wrong, proved insufficient to confirm the re-enfranchised citizens in their newly recovered status, and Solon invoked a new law of crime which vested the right of action in society; he permitted any Athenian citizen to prosecute for an attack upon the rights of his fellow.

It may be felt that I have overstated the importance of these elements in the Solonian reform, or have erred in regarding them as directed primarily toward the solution of this single problem, the rehabilitation of the body politic. Yet Aristotle fixed upon these same three measures—the prohibition against lending on the security of the debtor's person, the provision for criminal prosecution, and the institution of popular courts of original jurisdiction—as Solon's greatest contribution to the process that was to make Attica the cradle of democracy.[51]

[50] Ar. *Cons. Ath.* ix. 1; vii. 3.
[51] *Cons. Ath.* ix. 1.

CHAPTER V

SPECIAL FORMS OF CRIMINAL ACTION
IN ATTIC LAW

Solon's basic problems and their relationship to the institution of true criminal law, have been, for the most part, sufficiently established from the legislator's own words, and less authoritative sources have served chiefly to corroborate and to supply detail. But the attempt to determine precisely the form of his enactments and to reconstruct the subsequent history of criminal legislation must be prosecuted under less favorable conditions. Solon's poems naturally have nothing to say of particular laws or of the technical minutiae of legislation,[1] and, when the poems are left behind, there are scarcely any authentic sources until we come to the dramatic poets and the slight remains of early Attic prose. Yet there is one important storehouse of information that hitherto has been strangely neglected, and the task of sifting and testing the bits of information gleaned here and there in writings of a later age may well be deferred until certain implications of the Athenian legal vocabulary have been examined. These will be found to throw some light on the development of criminal process during the centuries preceding Solon's legislation.

Dike and graphe

One of the most obvious of these implications I have noted in an earlier study, where it is pointed out that the familiar distinction between graphe and dike, public action

[1] Linforth, 70.

and civil suit, bespeaks a "considerable time during which public actions were entered in writing, but private actions not."² This distinction further illustrates the order of historical sequence in which civil and criminal law usually are developed. Even in Homer, δίκη is found in the sense of "decision," "judgment,"³ while δικάζειν is used of one who pronounces, δικάζεσθαι of one who applies for, a judgment or decision.⁴ In the orators these are stereotyped expressions for the conduct of civil litigation, while γραφή, γράφεσθαι are in like manner habitually used of public or criminal actions as distinguished from civil suits.⁵ This would indicate, not only that the law and procedure governing private actions had become fairly extensive before the introduction of the graphe, but also that the development of criminal law was for the most part subsequent to the innovation. Thus the time at which public actions were first required to be entered in writing, if it can be determined, will set a probable anterior limit to the great age of expansion in the field of criminal law. The possibility which at once suggests itself, that Solon himself introduced the requirement, and criminal actions were entered in writing from the start, may be considered later when fuller data are at hand.⁶ This only can be said at present, either the written notation of criminal actions began at an early date, or the extension of criminal law to the various acts eventually classified as crimes proceeded somewhat slowly.

² "Oral and Written Pleading in Athenian Courts," *Trans. Am. Phil. Assoc.* L (1919), 178.

³ E.g., *Odyssey* xi. 570; iii. 244; *Iliad* xvi. 542; xviii. 508 (sometimes interpreted otherwise; cf. Bonner, *Class. Phil.* VI, 28 f.). That this sense of the word was familiar is shown by the compound δικασπόλος (*Iliad* i. 238; *Odyssey* xi. 186). The early history of δίκη, as well as many other words with legal implications, has been exhaustively studied by Hirzel, *Themis, Dike, und Verwandtes* (Leipzig, 1907) and more recently by Ehrenberg, *Die Rechtsidee im frühen Griechentum* (Leipzig, 1921), where abundant references to earlier works will be found. The present study is not primarily concerned with the disputes as to etymology and original meaning.

⁴ Active, *Iliad* xviii. 506; xxiii. 574; middle, *Odyssey* xi. 545; xii. 440.

⁵ *Trans. Am. Phil. Assoc., loc. cit.*; cf. Lipsius, *Recht*, 240, n. 9.

⁶ *Infra* 104 ff.

*The special forms
of action*

At this point some information may be sought in the terminology of the so-called special forms of public action.[7] These are εἰσαγγελία, προβολή, μήνυσις, processes starting with a denunciation or information laid before the council or assembly, or in a few instances before a magistrate; ἔνδειξις, ἀπαγωγή, ἐφήγησις, involving the summary arrest of offenders caught *in flagrante delicto*; φάσις and ἀπογραφή, declarations regarding the possession of contraband or of state property. No account need be taken here of two other special forms, δοκιμασία and εὔθυνα, which start as official inquests instituted in the course of administrative routine and do not necessarily lead to criminal prosecutions.[8]

Here are a considerable number of processes for the punishment of crime, distinguished from the graphe by peculiarities of procedure and terminology. As the initiation of a graphe is γράφεσθαι, so we find corresponding to these various forms of action εἰσαγγέλλειν, προβάλλεσθαι, μηνύειν, ἐνδεικνύναι, ἀπάγειν, ἐφηγεῖσθαι, φαίνειν, ἀπογράφειν or ἀπογράφεσθαι, and the familiar periphrases with ποιεῖσθαι.[9] Now it has just been observed that, during a period not yet precisely determined but subsequent to the introduction of the graphe,[10] the criminal law of Athens was being greatly expanded. In this process of expansion the graphe was so constantly prescribed as the mode of action that it became the typical criminal process and γραφή the generic term for criminal actions.[11] The conclusion to which this tends is

---

[7] Briefly described by Lipsius (*Recht*, 263 ff.).   [8] *Ibid.* 264.

[9] These are sufficiently illustrated by the passages cited in *Trans. Am. Phil. Assoc.*, 183 ff. It is interesting to note a tendency to use the active voice where a litigant acts on his own responsibility, the middle where he requests an official to take action (cf. *ibid.* 178 f.).

[10] In speaking of the times when written notations of actions unquestionably were required (*ibid.* 178 ff.), I shall use the word "graphe" as a synonym of "criminal action;" in referring to a time presumably anterior to that requirement, I shall use the expression "criminal action." In regard to the probable date of the change, cf. *infra* 105 f.

[11] *Supra* 58.

obvious.   Though it is well to shun the dangers of hasty generalization, we are justified at least in proposing for examination the view that many, perhaps most, of these special forms of action represent a development of criminal process prior to the extensive employment of the graphe.

So marked a preponderance of the graphe over other forms clearly attests the existence in Athens of a tendency toward uniformity in practice and terminology found in all judicial systems and chiefly in those of a mature character. This trend must have been especially strong upon occasions when the whole body of law, both substantive and adjective, was subjected to thoroughgoing revision, as in the year of Euclides. The fact that these special forms remained unaffected by the general tendency and even survived several drastic revisions, when this tendency must have been especially pronounced, would seem to indicate that they were already well established when the graphe entered upon its great expansion.

There is, however, another way of accounting for the existence of these forms.   Some of them, by reason of dealing with particular kinds of offenses in peculiarly effective ways, presented advantages that would amply justify their creation as supplementary actions even though a complete system of graphae were available.   Eisangelia and probole, for example, enabled the citizen who was prosecuting an influential man for a grave crime against the state to go into court with the support of the council or assembly,[12] or in some instances to get the case tried before the whole assembly.   In fact the state might prescribe whatever mode of procedure and trial it deemed most appropriate to the case in hand.[13]   Menysis enabled the council or assembly to receive informations regarding grave offenses from slaves or aliens who ordinarily were not entitled to initiate prosecutions.[14]   Such actions as

[12] Expressed by the adoption of a resolution (cf. Lipsius, *Recht*, 202), or even by the appointment of official prosecutors (*ibid.* 206, n. 97).
[13] *Ibid.* 176 ff.   [14] *Ibid.* 208 ff.

endeixis, apagoge, and the rarer ephegesis, which insured the summary arrest of the criminal,[15] were unquestionably more effective methods of dealing with certain heinous offenses than the ordinary graphe. Practically all the special actions involved the detention or binding over of the defendant for trial, which was not usual in regular criminal actions.[16] Even phasis and apographe were not without their distinctive characteristics; and none of the special forms could have been merged in the graphe without impairing to some extent the effectiveness of the criminal law. Thus we cannot determine upon general grounds whether it is more likely that these actions originated before the graphe and escaped assimilation by reason of the advantages they offered, or were introduced after or along with the graphe for the sake of these same advantages. They must be separately examined if the question is to be answered with any degree of assurance.

There is ample reason for regarding eisangelia as ancient. Long before the archonship of Solon the Areopagus exercised extensive judicial powers and dealt with grave offenses against the state.[17] These offenses must have been brought to the attention of the council by its members, or perhaps other individuals, for it is difficult to imagine how otherwise these functions could have been discharged. But such a proceeding, by whatever name one may wish to call it, is essentially what was termed eisangelia in the fifth and fourth centuries.[18] To believe that it was distinguished in the sixth century and earlier by some word which vanished utterly, for a reason unknown, and was later replaced by εἰσαγγελία, would be absurd; it becomes a mere quibble to

[15] *Ibid.* 317 ff.

[16] *Ibid.* 811 ff.

[17] Ar. *Cons. Ath.* iii. 6; cf. Lipsius, *Recht*, 12 ff.

[18] This is to be seen in the power of the council to impose fines up to the amount of 500 drachmas in eisangelia without reference to the assembly or the courts (Lipsius, *Recht*, 202). For the way in which the council inherited its criminal jurisdiction from the more ancient Council of the Areopagus, cf. *infra* 84 f.

deny that eisangelia is an ancient proceeding which originated probably in judicial functions exercised by the council
long before the time of Solon. This accords with the course
of development in the early treatment of crime observed by
Maine and with the analogies between eisangelia and the
Roman *privilegium* to which he calls attention.[19]   The procedure is exactly what might be expected to evolve from the
extremely primitive types of community action depicted in
the Homeric poems.[20]   Furthermore, the antiquity of eisangelia is indicated by its employment in the fifth century for
the punishment of offenses not specifically forbidden by
law,[21] which looks like a survival from times when written
law was unknown, and also to some extent by its resemb-
lances to the judicial procedure of the Spartan council.[22]
Again, despite the apparent absence in the pre-Solonian
period of any material limitations upon the judicial powers
of the Areopagus, there must have been occasions when it
saw fit to refer decisions to the assembly.   Consequently
there is no valid reason for believing that eisangelia in the
assembly, or even probole, was unknown before the time of
Solon.

So very ancient is the legal connotation of μηνύειν and
μήνυτρον that no hesitation need be felt in including menysis
also among the earliest methods devised by the state for
bringing offenders to justice.[23]

When we turn to apagoge, we do not need the analogies
which abound in the primitive institutions of every race to
tell us that we are dealing with a practice of great antiquity.
Summary seizure of a culprit found *in flagrante delicto* by
the intending prosecutor obviously goes back to those
primitive cultural stages in which self-help is the common
method of dealing with offenders.[24]   Nor is it likely that

[19] *Supra* 22f.   [20] *Supra* 21 f.   [21] Lipsius, *Recht*, 184 ff.   [22] Cf. Gilbert, 80; *infra* 112 f.
[23] Homeric *Hymn to Hermes*, 264, 364; cf. Bonner, *Class. Phil.* VII (1912), 19.
[24] See Gernet, "Sur l'exécution capitale," *Rev. Ét. Gr.* XXXVII (1924), 281 ff.

endeixis and ephegesis were much slower to appear, for the instinct that impelled a man to call upon friends or kinsmen for help in case of resistance would prompt a similar appeal to the power and authority of a superior. Let the social group once come to deem its leaders responsible for the protection of individual rights against aggression from within the group as well as from without, and the individual will be quick to perceive the advantage over simple self-help of calling upon his superiors to seize a culprit, or even conducting them to the place where he may be found.

Of these special forms of public action, then, the greater number are demonstrably of ancient origin. It should be noted further that they have to do almost exclusively with offenses of the sort that first came to be punished by the state, with wrongs that affect the community as a whole,[25] or particularly atrocious violations of public peace and good order,[26] or with cases in which the operation of the old law of tort left a victim without recourse.[27] Finally, the words by which they are designated, with the single exception of ἀπογραφή, evidently acquired their technical meaning in an age of oral procedure. In view of all this, there can be little doubt that the inference we were at first tempted to draw is correct and the special forms represent in the main a somewhat sporadic development of criminal process antecedent to the system of graphae.

Implications of
legal terms

Inasmuch as I have based a number of deductions upon the Athenian legal vocabulary and shall have occasion to do so again, it may be well here to invite attention to the remarkable way in which the whole evolutionary process,

---

[25] Offenses of this type were punished chiefly by eisangelia.

[26] These were occasion for summary arrest.

[27] E.g., the eisangelia in the court of the archon for maltreatment (cf. Lipsius, *Recht*, 264, 351 ff.).

beginning with the most primitive stages, is reflected in the nouns and verbs of legal action.[28] The entire field of historical and comparative jurisprudence may be searched without finding another opportunity for this sort of investigation so tempting or so profitable. Greece is not the only land in which we can trace the evolution of law from its most primitive stages to a highly developed, scientific system; but nowhere else is that system so truly the independent, homogeneous expression of a people who from first to last speak the same language and are actuated by a coherent succession of political ideals.

The most general terms for prosecution and defense at law are the verbs διώκειν and φεύγειν, "to pursue" and "to flee;" plaintiff and defendant are accordingly ὁ διώκων and ὁ φεύγων. Here obviously we have reflected the most primitive method of dealing with wrongs and disputes, self-help, which ranged from cases in which a man pursued alone or with a few followers to those in which he called out the whole countryside to aid in punishing some act of violence, as in the "hue and cry" of early English times.[29]   The persistence of these terms, which is not paralleled in Roman or in English law, indicates that actual self-help gave way only very gradually to other methods of settling disputes or getting redress for wrongs.   Apparently these were voluntarily substituted in practice by disputants from considerations of expediency; their experimental stage—if so it may be called—lasted longer than would have been the case had they been taken over from a more highly developed culture or arbitrarily imposed by a sovereign.[30]   This accords with

    [28] Cf. Ehrenberg, 80, n. 1, with references.   Many of the words discussed in the present chapter have been studied by Ehrenberg, Hirzel, and others, but usually from a different point of view and with more attention to the history of ideas than of actual procedure.

    [29] Cf. Pollock and Maitland, *History of English Law* (Cambridge, 1899), II, 578 ff.

    [30] Cf. the suppression of self-help in England by the crown (*ibid.* II, 574 ff., 579); this tendency is to be seen even before the Norman conquest (*ibid.* II, 453 ff.).

what little is known of the development of civil process in Greece through voluntary arbitration; in the earlier stages the parties to the arbitration were always potentially, and might at any moment become actually, pursuer and pursued. The quasi-legal connotations of τιμωρός and τιμωρεῖν also probably go back to the age of self-help.[31]

Although we are tempted to see in ἀγών, the most general term for any sort of trial at law, an echo from the stage, intermediate between self-help and true legal processes, in which disputes are settled by single combat, the history of the word is too complicated to warrant an attempt at positive conclusions.[32] In any event the traces of trial by combat are so very few and doubtful that the practice seems not to have had an important part in the evolution of law among the Greeks.[33]

The uses of δίκη and the corresponding verbs are too familiar to require further discussion. The body of law in connection with which these words acquired their technical meanings was gradually taking form during a long period of time, and, it must be remembered, included not merely civil law in the proper sense, but also, until at least the time of Solon, a great mass of penal rules which were eventually interwoven into the true criminal law and went to swell the number of graphae.

[31] Cf. τιμή="compensation," "penalty" in Homer, especially *Iliad* i. 159: ἱμὴν ἀρνύμενοι.

[32] The word originally refers to a concourse, gathering, and there is no reason to believe that it was applied to the throng that collected to witness a trial by combat any more than to such an assemblage as is described in the trial scene (*Iliad* xviii. 497 ff.) looking on at an arbitration (cf. Hesiod, *Works*, 28 ff.; *Theog.*, 84 ff.). A different opinion is held by Glotz (277 ff.).

[33] The tenuous character of the evidence for trial by combat among the Greeks, except in the case of international disputes, may be seen from the discussion of Glotz, *loc. cit.* One is impressed by the fondness the Greeks evince from the very first for rational discussion as a means of settling disputes; the agora and the themistes are what chiefly distinguish the primitive Hellenic culture from that of the races round about them. The idea of a divine decision, which underlies all ordeals, seems soon to have been overshadowed in the minds of the Greeks by their interest in the human and secular part. Thus the evidentiary oath soon lost its associations with divine judgment; cf. Smith, *Hesiod to Solon*, chap. 5.

On the side of criminal law a concurrent trend of development is attested, as we have just seen, by the phraseology of the special forms of action. Another word which throws light on this early period is κατήγορος, with the corresponding verb κατηγορεῖν. It is clear that κατήγορος is closely connected with καταγορεύειν, to "speak against" in a public gathering, and that κατηγορεῖν is a denominative, formed when the noun has acquired its special meaning. Even as late as the fourth century these words are chiefly used of criminal prosecutions;[34] when not so used they are employed for the most part in a very general or in a figurative sense.[35] The preponderant element in their connotation comes from the criminal law, a circumstance which seems to speak for the long duration and importance of the criminal jurisdiction exercised by deliberative bodies, particularly the Areopagus, and to support the view that eisangelia is a very ancient form.

Outlawry and
legalized self-help

There is still another archaic formula met with here and there as late as the fourth century, in which we can trace the development of two ancient and universal processes for dealing with crime—outlawry and legalized self-help. This is νηποινεὶ τεθνάναι and its virtual equivalent ἄτιμον τεθνάναι.[36] Both expressions confer a legal right to take human life; in the historic period they have come to denote merely a justi-

[34] Cf. Dem. xix. 2, 257, 275; xxi. 5, 64; xxii. 66; xxiii. 96; xxiv. 62, 173; lviii. 69; xxv. 3–4; for the verb, cf. xxi. 5, 64; lvii. 26; xix. 257. Such instances can be presented in any number.

[35] For example, "to be one's own accuser" (Dem. xlv. 2, 23, 40).

[36] Cf. Dem. xxiii. 60, from which it has been possible to restore the text of the inscription containing the ancient law on homicide (*CIA* I, 61, lines 37 ff.). The formula is found in decrees of the fifth and following centuries (And. i. 95 ff.; *CIG* 2008; cf. Plato *Laws* 874C, and the more expanded formula in an inscription from Eretria, *RIJG* ix, lines 32 ff., 56 ff.). Demosthenes comments on the ancient meaning of ἄτιμος (ix. 44; cf. note following). The instances in which the right to slay is conferred upon the whole community (outlawry) are quite distinct from those in which the law authorizes action by the individual or group directly affected by the wrong (ordinary self-help); this will appear in the course of the argument.

fiable or excusable homicide, but it is obvious that they are a creation of those times when the taking of human life was atoned by the payment of blood-money, and referred originally to homicides for which the blood-price (τιμή, ποινή) could not be exacted.[37]

Among the Greeks of the heroic age, as in other primitive societies, the individual depended for personal security chiefly upon the compensation which would be demanded by his family, in the event of his being slain, from the family of the slayer. There were, however, certain circumstances in which the life of a freeman might be taken without entailing the payment of the blood-price. He might be an alien wanderer, with no relatives at hand to demand the atonement;[38] he might have been expelled and disowned by his family or tribal group;[39] or he might be slain by way of retribution for some offense which the members of his family would regard as making his life justly a forfeit to the injured person.[40] We may now inquire what elements in the legal institutions of a later age were evolved from these exceptions.

[37] Cf. *Recueil* II, 49. This sense of ἄτιμος is clearly distinguished by Swoboda in his "Beiträge zur griechischen Rechtsgeschichte," *Ztschr. Sav. St.* (Rom.) XXVI (1905), 149 ff. The arguments for and against this interpretation of these and other passages are briefly reviewed by Usteri, *Aechtung und Verbannung im griechischen Recht* (Berlin, 1903), 12, n. 1.) Although the word is found in the more familiar sense as early as Homer (*Iliad* i. 171; xvi. 90), we can scarcely doubt that the original meaning is "that on which no price is set," for which no payment is exacted. The etymology of ποινή and τιμή is discussed exhaustively by Glotz (*Solidarité*, 101 ff.).

[38] This is the ἀτίμητος μετανάστης of *Iliad* ix. 648 and xvi. 59, who might be outraged and oppressed with impunity.

[39] Cf. the language used by Nestor of the man who is guilty of fostering civil strife (*Iliad* ix. 63; cf. *supra* 21). This primitive mode of punishment is discussed by Glotz (*Solidarité*, 22 ff.); in my opinion, however, some of his instances might better be put in other categories and this reserved for cases in which an offense against the group is punished.

[40] Although no actual instance of noxal surrender is described by Homer, so far as I can discover, we cannot account for the development of legalized self-help without assuming that it was a practice of the early Hellenes, in common with other primitive peoples. On the noxal surrender in early Roman society, cf. Strachan-Davidson I, 38–39. Two motives must be distinguished here, inability and disinclination to protect a culprit (cf. *infra* 70, n. 49). Glotz discusses the subject, with copious illustration from other primitive societies (*Solidarité*, 171 ff.), but here again seems to me to admit cases which properly belong under other heads (e.g., 172, n. 2).

With the treatment of the alien we are here but slightly concerned; its later history is not primarily connected with the criminal law, but rather with the practice of clientage and with the legislation by which the state, as it increased its authority, established and defined the rights and status of aliens.

The second exception, however, is closely related to the objects of our inquiry. The primitive punishment of expulsion for an offense against the group developed with the lapse of time and the growth of the community into the decree of outlawry, which made of the criminal a "wolf's head," whose life might be taken by any man without fear of punishment or reprisal. In later times a sentence of this kind was officially pronounced by the Athenians against any who might attempt to overthrow the government, together with their accessories,[41] and against homicides who might return unlawfully into the country after having been banished by the courts.[42]   In the case of most offenses against the state this primitive mode of punishment gave place to penalties inflicted by the government upon conviction in a court of justice. Its retention in the two instances noted is probably to be accounted for by the fear and abhorrence with which the Greeks regarded tyranny and by the quasi-religious character of the laws concerning homicide.[43]

[41] And. i. 95 ff.; Ar. *Cons. Ath.* xvi. 10; Dem. ix. 43 f.; *CIG* 2008; *RIJG* ix. 32 ff., 56 ff.; xxii. For a complete discussion of the subject, cf. *Recueil* I, 47 ff., and Usteri's exhaustive study of exile (cf. *supra* 67, n. 37).

[42] Dem. xxiii. 28; *CIA* I. 61. 30 ff. Dr. Smith ("Early Greek Codes," *Class. Phil.* XVII [1922], 197) seems to regard this provision as a device of Dracon, from which Solon may have got the idea of the public action. But it is in reality a custom that antedates by centuries the legislation of Dracon. The circumstances which led Solon to the institution of the criminal action, and the probability that the process was modeled upon the old action in tort rather than upon the archaic special forms of criminal action or the practice of outlawry, will be examined in detail in the following chapters.

[43] On the peculiar abhorrence entertained by the Greek constitutional states for tyranny, cf. *Recueil* II, 34 ff. On religion as a factor in the retardation of legal progress, cf. *supra* 11.

The third exception is really the most interesting to the student of legal history, yet slight attention has been given, so far as I can discover, to its most important implications. It represents the efforts of primitive society to reconcile two principles which were equally fundamental and bound inevitably to conflict—self-help and the blood-feud.[44] How is the right of the slain man's kindred to the blood-price to be adjusted to the right by which a man slays the adulterer or the robber taken *in flagrante delicto?* It can hardly be doubted that the solution resulted eventually from the recurrence of particular instances in which a claim for vengeance or blood-money was contested on the basis of the right to self-help and was finally abandoned by the kindred of the slain man; after many cases had been so adjusted, a custom would be created which would recognize the right to take life under certain circumstances without becoming liable to the usual penalties.

How a case of this kind might be dealt with prior to the formation of definite custom may perhaps be illustrated from the slaying of the suitors in the *Odyssey.* The situation which confronts Telemachus and Odysseus is clearly one for which there is no close precedent; it is exceptional by reason of the number of offenders as well as the justification for their conduct which is sought in their status as suitors for the hand of the queen. Hence Telemachus addresses to them a formal protest and warning, at first in his palace and again in the full assembly of the folk. He bids them depart from his abode, solemnly calling the gods to witness that, if they persist in this wasting of his property without atonement, their deaths, should Zeus grant him

[44] I have not made an exhaustive search for discussions of this conflict, but note that it is passed over by Strachan-Davidson (*Problems of the Roman Criminal Law*, chap. 3), Leist (*Gräco-italische Rechtsgeschichte* II, chap. 3), Thonissen (*Droit criminel de la Grèce légendaire*), and others. Yet it seems to me a very real problem and an interesting one, and nowhere can it be studied to greater advantage than in the Greek sources.

retribution, shall be without atonement.⁴⁵ In the moment of vengeance, Odysseus enumerates the wrongs which justify him in demanding the lives of the offenders: they have wasted his property; they have debauched his female slaves; they have treacherously wooed his wife, while he is yet living; they fear neither the gods nor the condemnation of men.⁴⁶ When his bloody revenge becomes known, the majority of the Ithacans, urged on by Eupithes, resolve to avenge their slain kinsmen, but they are repulsed and the ringleader slain.⁴⁷ Finally, by the direction of Zeus, the goddess Athena brings about a covenant whereby the slaying of the suitors is forgiven and forgotten and peace reestablished between the house of Odysseus and the kindred of the slain.⁴⁸

How rapidly the various acts for which the life of the offender might be taken without retaliation were defined by custom, we cannot say.⁴⁹ The older Attic law, however,

⁴⁵ *Odyssey* i. 374 ff., especially 380:

νήποινοί κεν ἔπειτα δόμων ἔντοσθεν ὄλοισθε.

cf. *ibid.* ii. 139 ff.

⁴⁶ *Ibid.* xxii. 35 ff. The emphasis throughout the narrative on the debauching of the maidservants, and the fact that those among them who have been unchaste are actually slain (*ibid.* 417–73), strongly suggest that custom already sanctions the killing of anyone who debauches a woman of the household, whether bond or free (on legalized self-help in the case of a concubine in later times, cf. Dem. xxiii. 53). As has been said, it is probably the number and influence of the offenders, and their alleged status as suitors, that make the situation exceptional.

⁴⁷ *Ibid.* xxiv. 413 ff. Although Eupithes represents the vengeance of Odysseus as a great public injury (cf. *supra* 21 f.), he also appeals to his hearers on the score of their duty to avenge the slaying of their kinsmen (*ibid.* 433 ff.).

⁴⁸ *Ibid.* 472 ff., especially 482 ff.:

ἐπεὶ δὴ μνηστῆρας ἐτίσατο δῖος Ὀδυσσεύς,
ὅρκια πιστὰ ταμόντες ὁ μὲν βασιλευέτω αἰεί,
ἡμεῖς δ᾽αὖ παίδων τε κασιγνήτων τε φόνοιο
ἔκλησιν θέωμεν· τοὶ δ᾽ἀλλήλους φιλεόντων
ὡς τὸ πάρος, πλοῦτος δὲ καὶ εἰρήνη ἅλις ἔστω.

⁴⁹ The process must have been an irregular one, as many variable factors entered in. We have to take account of the two motives for the noxal surrender, disinclination to protect the culprit and actual inability. Again, even after custom had begun to sanction the killing of an offender, there must have been cases in which a powerful group refused to admit the claim based on self-help. The noxal surrender is usually treated as the result solely of inability to protect an offender (Strachan-Davidson, 38 f.). Glotz (*Solidarité*, 171) notes the possibility that the other motive may be present, but does not attempt to develop it, or to trace its connection with legalized self-help.

contained a number of provisions relating to justifiable homicide which appear to be the outgrowth of this ancient exception. The nocturnal housebreaker, the robber, the adulterer caught in *flagrante delicto*, could be slain with impunity.[50] Although in some of these cases it may have been the intention of the law to provide for the exercise of self-defense, rather than self-help,[51] in others, as for example adultery, we have beyond question legalized self-help, in which the slaying is not a defensive measure but a punishment.[52] It may be noted, moreover, that the law contemplates action by the injured person, or his near kin, and that these provisions which legalize self-help, unlike the decree of outlawry, are to be associated with the ancient law of tort rather than with state prosecution of crime.[53]

So far as we can discover, then, the various processes which the state had developed for the punishment of crimes prior to Solon's legislation were limited to the special forms of action previously discussed and the ancient practice of outlawry. It can scarcely be doubted that all or most of them existed from a very early time throughout the whole area of Hellenic civilization, and that they represent a common stock of Hellenic notions and practices having to do with the punishment of crime.[54]

[50] Lipsius, *Recht*, 615 f.; similar provisions are found in Plato's *Laws* (874B-C).

[51] For example the provision ἀμυνόμενος or εὐθὺς ἀμυνόμενος (Dem. xxiii. 60).

[52] This is clear from the treatment authorized (Lys. i. 49; cf. the defendant's statements of fact throughout the speech).

[53] Cf., for example, Plato *Laws* 874B-C.

[54] On the form in which they are found in Sparta and Crete, cf. *infra* 111 ff.

CHAPTER VI

FORM AND SCOPE OF SOLON'S CRIMINAL LEGISLATION

The more particular inquiries which relate to the details of Solon's enactment at once suggest some exceedingly interesting questions. In what form did Solon's brilliant solution of the problem of crime come to him? Was the fundamental principle that certain attacks upon the individual are a source of evil to the state, and must be dealt with by the state, revealed to him in a flash of sudden inspiration? Or, when he set about formulating laws designed to stop particular abuses, did he find that certain offenses, by their very nature, could not be adequately repressed under the old law of tort? Why did he introduce a new type of criminal action, modeled upon the old action for tort? Why was he not content with the traditional forms, which, as we have seen, had existed long before his time? We may reasonably expect to find the processes by which he reached his solution reflected to some extent in the form of his enactments. Did he draw up a general law determining the right of action in the prosecution of all offenses which he proposed to treat as crimes? Or, in framing statutes which dealt with specific offenses, did he insert a clause conferring the right of action upon all citizens in each several instance where he deemed it necessary? These questions may appear at first to be directed to matters merely of petty detail, inviting to the exercise of academic ingenuity. When studied more carefully they will be found to have a very definite bearing upon the proper understanding of our larger subject. In fact, when we see how much light the prosecution of these inquiries will throw upon Solon's work and its affinities with later legislation, we shall wonder that they have been so long passed over in silence.

*The form of
Solon's enactment*

Since Solon alludes to his legislation only in the most general terms, we are dependent upon the brief statements of Aristotle and Plutarch for the little explicit information we have regarding the institution of the public action. At first glance it seems clear that the nomothete enacted the provision for criminal prosecution in a single law designed to cover all cases. Plutarch actually speaks of "this law,"[1] and Aristotle brackets it with two other measures in such a way as to give distinctly the impression that it was contained in a single statute.[2] The view these passages suggest has not, so far as I am aware, been subjected to critical analysis, although a number of serious difficulties are involved.

Assuming for the moment that both writers have in mind the text of a general law covering all cases, it is obvious that both cannot be quoting, so dissimilar is their language. However, let us say for the sake of argument that one of them—we do not yet know which—is quoting this law, perhaps from an Atthidograph,[3] and the other independently paraphrasing. Aristotle's words are τὸ ἐξεῖναι τῷ βουλομένῳ τιμωρεῖν ὑπὲρ τῶν ἀδικουμένων. We feel at once that τιμωρεῖν and ὑπὲρ τῶν ἀδικουμένων are hardly appropriate to the wording of a law which sets up a definite procedure for the prosecution of definite offenses; under a statute so vague one might have proceeded in any way he chose on the ground of any conceivable injury. Only ἐξεῖναι τῷ βουλομένῳ can be taken

[1] *Solon* xviii *fin.*   [2] *Cons. Ath.* ix. 1.   [3] Busolt II, 283, n. 3.

as verbatim quotation from a law, and the rest would appear to be Aristotle's paraphrase. Turning to Plutarch we find παντὶ λαβεῖν δίκην ὑπὲρ τοῦ κακῶς πεπονθότος ἔδωκε· καὶ γὰρ πληγέντος ἑτέρου καὶ βιασθέντος ἢ βλαβέντος ἐξῆν τῷ δυναμένῳ καὶ βουλομένῳ γράφεσθαι τὸν ἀδικοῦντα καὶ διώκειν. Here again very little sounds like quotation from a statute; the greater part is paraphrase, exegesis, or mere repetition. Three examples of crimes—and not very good ones at that[4]— illustrate ὑπὲρ τοῦ κακῶς πεπονθότος, which corresponds to Aristotle's ὑπὲρ τῶν ἀδικουμένων. The words ἐξῆν τῷ . . . . βουλομένῳ γράφεσθαι τὸν ἀδικοῦντα may very well be quoted, and perhaps καὶ διώκειν as well. If our authors are indeed reporting a blanket enactment in which Solon defined or enumerated the acts that were to be subject to criminal prosecution, they have failed to give us what we should most like to have, the legislator's definition or enumeration of crimes. The few words that can be accepted as quotation, ἐξεῖναι (ἐξῆν) τῷ βουλομένῳ (γράφεσθαι, κτλ.) give not the slightest hint toward the solution of our problem. Their source may equally well be a single law or many different laws, in fact they are likely to have had no other basis than familiarity with the criminal law of the fifth and fourth centuries, where γραψάσθω ὁ βουλόμενος Ἀθηναίων οἷς ἔξεστιν, or a similar clause, appears repeatedly in criminal statutes.[5]

If Solon really undertook to prescribe the manner of criminal prosecution in a single law, there were only two ways in which he could effectively limit its application to acts he regarded as crimes. He might seek to define crime by a word or phrase that would include all offenses against the public peace and good order and exclude those that

---

[4] Plutarch naturally thinks first of acts of violence (other than homicide) against individuals, but his language suggests the δίκαι αἰκείας (the usual action for simple assault; cf. Lipsius, Recht, 643 ff.), βιαίων (Dem. xxi. 44; cf. Recht, 637 ff.), βλάβης (ibid. 43; cf. Recht, 652 ff.), which are all private actions, rather than the γραφὴ ὕβρεως (Dem. xxi.¦47: ἐάν τις ὑβρίσῃ εἴς τινα . . . . ἢ παράνομόν τι ποιήσῃ, κτλ.), the criminal action for offenses of this character; cf. Recht, 420 ff.

[5] See Lipsius, Recht, 244, n. 16.

affected only individual rights.   Or he might categorically
enumerate all acts that were to be cause for criminal prosecution.   The first hypothesis involves an assumption 'that is
inherently improbable; it is unlikely that Solon, with all his
undoubted ability, was so far ahead of his time in habits of
thought as to entertain the predilection for general concepts
implied in this approach to the problem.   We should expect
to find him absorbed in the attempt to deal with particular
crimes in a somewhat practical way rather than in the quest
for a general formula.   Furthermore, adherence to this
hypothesis would commit us to the belief that the nomothete
achieved what the best thought of succeeding ages has not
produced, a formulation of the concept of crime sufficiently
precise to be self-determining in its application to particular
crimes;⁶ and that this most remarkable achievement then
vanished so completely as to leave not a trace of its existence
in the laws or judicial phraseology of the fifth and fourth
centuries.⁷   The other possibility, that Solon enumerated in
a general law the acts to be punished as crimes, is scarcely
more acceptable, if he placed any considerable number of
offenses in the new category.   A statute of this type would

⁶ The validity of the various definitions of crime recognized in modern systems
of law is the product of a long process of definition, classification, and drawing of
nice distinctions, both in legislation and the decisions of courts.   This is illustrated
by the different classifications that have prevailed in English law at various periods
(see Pollock and Maitland II, 511 ff.), and those found in Continental penal codes.
A definition of crime that will satisfy the logician or the student of general phil-
osophy will require to be redefined and interpreted by legislative enactment or
judicial pronouncement in practically every application to a specific class of
offenses.   "Even at the present moment we can hardly say that crime is one of
the technical terms of our law."   (Ibid. 573, n. 6; cf. Stephen, Hist. Crim. Law I,
1–5.)

⁷ We find no word or phrase comprising only offenses that give rise to criminal
actions as distinguished from private wrongs, though there are several expressions
that refer peculiarly to criminal actions, e.g., γραφή = ἀγὼν δημόσιος, δίκη δημοσία,
etc. (cf. Lipsius, Recht, 238 ff.).   Such words as ἀδίκημα, κακούργημα, παράνομον, etc.,
any one of which might have acquired a precise judicial implication had Solon or a
subsequent legislator employed it arbitrarily as a definition of crime (cf. infra 76,
n. 9), continued to be used with a moral, not a judicial, connotation that never
coincides with the distinction between crimes and civil wrongs.   Greek has no
word comparable to our "crime"; γραφή did not undergo the last stage of development that would have enriched the language by a convenient general term.

be an awkward thing at best, and, if it were not to give rise constantly to questions touching its scope and intent, would have to be a faithful, practically a verbatim, repetition from the separate enactments of all clauses in which crimes were defined and forbidden. The lawgiver could not well have put it into final form before he had completed the whole work of legislation and decided finally in each instance what acts were to be regarded as crimes and what viewed as infringements of private rights. Furthermore, such a law would have to be amended whenever a new criminal statute was enacted or an existing statute repealed—no trivial matter when laws were published on stone, or metal, or on wooden tablets. It is surely the height of absurdity to believe that Solon enacted a number of laws forbidding certain acts, prescribing penalties to be imposed, and specifying what magistrate was to have jurisdiction in each instance,[8] but containing no information as to how they were to be enforced; and that he then drew up a separate statute in which all these offenses were recapitulated at great length, merely for the purpose of stating that any citizen might prosecute. The conclusion is so obvious that it may well be asked why it has seemed necessary to demonstrate it in such detail.[9] The reason is that the hypothesis of a single law

[8] Penalties and jurisdiction, which were not the same in all cases, must have been separately prescribed in laws concerning different offenses, as was customary in the fifth and fourth centuries (e.g., Dem. xxi. 47; cf. Ant. v. 9 ff., where various laws are contrasted). This practice evidently is derived from ancient usage (cf. following note).

[9] It may be objected that Solon, although he could not have formulated a definition of crime that would be self-determining, might have (1) arbitrarily defined crimes by a word or phrase and then enacted a law prescribing the right of action for all cases so defined, or (2) cast his criminal statutes in the form of prohibitions and then prescribed the right of action for all prohibited acts. Neither hypothesis is tenable, in my opinion. A definition of crime, or a form of criminal statute, which had once been established in a considerable body of legislation could scarcely have disappeared so completely, before two centuries had passed, as to leave no trace of its existence in the forms or phraseology of Attic law. On the other hand, we have the famous fragment from the laws on homicide ascribed to Dracon (*CIA* I. 61), which preserves formulas of unquestioned antiquity, presumably pre-Solonian. Here we find the ἐάν τις clause that is the prevailing form in the fourth century. We may reasonably believe that the formula used before

determining the right of action for all criminal cases, although it commits us to the belief that Solon did either an impossible or a hopelessly stupid thing, is tacitly accepted, when not explicitly stated, in every account of his legislation that has come under my notice.   So far as I can discover, no one has hitherto given it the slight measure of attention that suffices to reveal its absurdity.

Up to this point our attempt at analysis has had to do with general, technical considerations such as are involved in the proper arrangement of any considerable body of substantive law with its necessary adjective regulations.   It has pointed unmistakably to the probability that Solon followed the simple method familiar to us from the law of the fifth and fourth centuries, and incorporated in each criminal statute, along with the sections relating to jurisdiction and penalties, a clause granting the right of action to any citizen. The soundness of this conclusion may now be tested by examining the definite problems involved in the handling of particular offenses.

*Invention of the
criminal action*

Two of the many laws traditionally ascribed to Solon, and two only, can be accepted unhesitatingly as the authentic work of the great nomothete, one of them the enactment that abolished slavery for debt, the other the law forbidding parents to sell their children as slaves.[10]   Both lay very near to the essential and insistent problem of maintaining the integrity of the burgess body and preventing Athenian

Solon's time and almost unvaryingly afterward is the one he employed: "If any-one (whosoever) . . . . let any Athenian prosecute in the court of the . . . . and in case of conviction . . . . ."   The wide use of this formula in early times is indicated by its frequent occurrence in Cretan inscriptions which, though probably of the fifth century, represent a less advanced state than Athenian laws of the same period (e.g., *RIJG*, xvii-xix *passim*).   See also an Elean rhetra (Michel, 195; cf. Michel, 1 and 196, and Herondas ii. 45 ff., 50 ff.).   General prohibitions and commands appear, but wherever it is needful to qualify or to specify acts, we are likely to meet the conditional clause.

[10] *Supra* 55.

citizens from being degraded to slavery by economic necessity, a problem that appears to have been constantly present to Solon's thought during the course of his legislative activity.[11]

Let us imagine that Solon has just drawn up the substantive portion of the law forbidding the sale of a child by a parent, and is about to define the proper jurisdiction and fix the penalty. He is dealing with an attack upon an individual of the sort that hitherto have been dealt with as torts and not punished as crimes. Could a man of his acumen have failed to perceive that under the existing system of private actions based upon the old law of tort the right of action upon a violation of the statute would be vested solely in the offender himself, and that the prohibition he had just drawn so carefully could not be enforced, for want of a prosecutor? What solution could be simpler or would more readily suggest itself than the insertion of a clause extending to any citizen the right to institute a prosecution?

The enactment, or enactments, by which Solon abolished slavery for debt present somewhat similar difficulties. Aristotle and Plutarch speak as though the legislator prohibited lending upon the security of the person;[12] on the other hand Gilliard seems to regard the prohibition as addressed to the borrower, who is forbidden to offer his person as security.[13] The assumption that underlies these points of view may be discerned in every discussion of this act of Solon's; it is invariably taken for granted that the lawgiver's task was to put a stop to contracts in which loans were made upon the security of the person and that, when this was done, slavery for debt was *ipso facto* abolished. This we have good reason to doubt. Lending on the

[11] *Supra* 55.   [12] *Cons. Ath.* vi. 1; ix. 1; Plut. *Solon* xv *med.*

[13] 175 ff., especially 177: "En défendant que dorénavant un débiteur engageât son corps . . . . ."

security of the person was manifestly a common practice, founded upon general custom of long standing. We cannot for a moment believe that the right to seize the person must be created by a specific agreement entered into when an obligation was contracted; we must rather conclude that any monetary obligation could be enforced by seizure of the debtor's person in default of other security or property sufficient to satisfy the debt.[14] (In these circumstances what was needed, and what Solon must have enacted, was a law specifically forbidding the seizure of the debtor's person.) This may have been supplemental to the prohibition we have discussed, or possibly to a law depriving creditors who lent upon the security of the person of the right to sue for recovery of loans,[15] but it was absolutely essential to the abolition of slavery for debt.[16] And such a law, like the prohibition against the sale of a child by a parent, could not well have been enforced by civil action. An Athenian who had once been seized as a slave by his creditor found himself in a plight that offered little prospect of successful recourse to law on his part. If the right of action were restricted to the injured party, the law was virtually a nullity.[17] As in the preceding instance, the simplest and most natural way of meeting the difficulty was to insert a clause which would enable any citizen to prosecute. In fact one is strongly

[14] This seems to have been a universal practice in the ancient world; in other Greek states than Athens it persisted for many centuries (Beauchet, *Histoire du droit privé de la république athénienne* II, 414 f.; III, 204 f.).

[15] For an analogous provision cf. [Dem.] xxxv. 51.

[16] That Solon's legislation on the subject, whatever its nature, did abolish slavery for debt cannot reasonably be doubted. Cf. Gilliard, 175 f.

[17] It was to meet this difficulty that the venerable proceeding called in Athens τὸ ἀφαιρεῖσθαι εἰς ἐλευθερίαν was devised, apparently at a very remote time. In the laws of Gortyna (*col.* xi. 24–25) we find a provision that every citizen is to afford comfort to anyone who is being seized without a judgment of court (cf. *Recueil* I, 446). Though we have here a germ of criminal law, the part of the citizen in this primitive proceeding does not extend to the punishment of the offender; compensation for the wrong would doubtless be sought by the victim after his release if there were a prospect of successful litigation. Solon, on the other hand, must have provided a penalty, as in the case of other offenses to be punished by the state.

tempted to believe that public prosecution of those who attempt to reduce Athenian citizens to slavery goes back to this law of Solon.[18]

The scope of
Solon's criminal law

There must have been other offenses against which Solon undertook to legislate that presented the same difficulties and were dealt with in the same way. We may also believe that, when this simple and effective procedure had once been adapted to the public action, Solon saw the advantage of employing it in the prosecution of still other crimes, which hitherto had been punishable only by processes not readily available to the ordinary citizen.[19]   This brings up the truly important questions that have to do with the general character and scope of his criminal legislation. As a preliminary to their consideration, it may be well to go back and take stock of what we have been able to discover touching his problems and his ways of meeting them.

In studying the lyric poets, we observed that the conception of crime which was gradually developed in the eighth and seventh centuries found its fullest expression in a poem of Solon composed before the archonship.[20]   This interest of the future nomothete in the problems of crime and punishment, if we may judge from his choice of examples in the extant fragments, was still focused primarily upon the greater offenses which affected immediately and patently the state as a whole. They were the acts whose criminal character was easily to be recognized from an inspection of general social and political conditions. But we cannot escape the conclusion that Solon's theories regarding crime

---

[18] There is no certain evidence of a γραφὴ ἀνδραποδισμοῦ in Attic law, though it is found in Plato's *Laws* (955A; cf. 879A); kidnapers caught in the act were prosecuted by ἀπαγωγή in the court of the Eleven and could be punished by death if convicted (*Recht*, 320 f.).

[19] *Infra* 82.   [20] *Supra* 37 ff.

were materially influenced by his actual experiences as a legislator. In dealing with specific abuses and enacting measures for their repression, finding himself repeatedly confronted by such difficulties as are exhibited in the two instances just discussed, he must have come to a truer understanding of the nature and functions of criminal legislation as well as its detailed application. So thoughtful a man as Solon could not have struggled with these practical difficulties of procedure for long without coming to realize that they were but outward and visible signs of a fundamental difference which sets apart certain types of offenses against the individual from ordinary invasions of purely personal rights. By the time he had completed his task, he must have been well aware that many acts which, directly, affect the individual rather than the community are, in their last analysis, crimes, and must be dealt with by the state.

This is not to say that Solon plumbed all the depths of his problem, or brought into being a system of criminal law that was perfect and complete either in general theory or in its detailed application. We cannot believe that the sum total of his enactments was at all comparable to the criminal law of the later fifth and the fourth centuries. Without taking account of the additions that were made in connection with the reforms of Ephialtes,[21] or of the fact that the body of law which passed traditionally for Solon's at the end of the fifth century was found to require supplementary legislation,[22] we can readily understand that the performance of the legislator was limited by the political and intellectual state of his time, a time when the process that was to culminate in the Athenian democracy was barely beginning.

If we undertake an inquiry into the details of Solon's criminal legislation, we are reduced to conjecture. But the facts that have been developed regarding his principal aims and methods and some of his difficulties appear to justify

[21] *Infra* 100 ff.   [22] And. i. [83].

certain conclusions as to the general types of offenses dealt with in this first criminal code of the Western world. First come acts involving the unmerited degradation of Athenians from citizenship. These may be set down with little hesitation, not only because of our having two undoubted examples in the statutes against seizure for debt and the sale of children, but because we know that Solon looked upon the decay of the burgess body as the greatest and most immediate danger to the state and its rehabilitation as his most urgent task.[23] Next may be put other attacks upon individuals which could not be adequately repressed under the earlier system of private actions, in which the right to prosecute was restricted to the injured person. Several of the actions for maltreatment (κακώσεως), which Glotz[24] regards as the earliest examples of criminal action and consequently attributes to Solon, have to do with offenses of this type. While we cannot of course be certain that Solon applied this principle in other instances than the two we know, it is not improbable that he did so, and that some if not all of the actions for maltreatment were created by his statutes.[25]

Lastly we come to those offenses which the state already punished as crimes by means of special forms of action.[26] Most of these special forms, like eisangelia, menysis, and probably phasis, could be prosecuted successfully only by or with the support of men whose influence was sufficient to secure a majority of votes in the aristocratic council; unquestionably they were not readily available to the ordinary citizen. Even those actions which could be instituted before a magistrate and decided without reference to the council,

[23] Supra 55.   [24] Solidarité, 371.

[25] Maltreatment of orphans and heiresses could be prosecuted by eisangelia before the archon (cf. supra 63, n. 27). This, like the summary process against kidnapers (supra 80, n. 18), and the vindication of freedom (supra 79, n. 17), appears to have been an attempt to bolster up the old law of tort at one of its weak points. Cf. infra 110 f.

[26] On these special forms and the reasons for regarding them as a sporadic development of criminal process anterior to the legislation of Solon, cf. supra 61 ff.

such as apagoge, had probably not yet developed into criminal actions in the proper sense. It must be remembered that they were devised in very early times, when the conception of crime virtually did not exist and even the most flagrant wrongs against individuals were invariably dealt with as torts.[27] In practice and custom they must have been instituted almost without exception by the injured individual or a near relative, and it is highly probable that it was only after the legislation of Solon had emphasized the principle of criminal prosecution and made it familiar to the citizens, that they came to be thought of as inviting any and every citizen to prosecute for wrongs against others. The mere fact that Solon found it necessary to adapt the simpler process of the law of tort to the punishment of crime indicates that these customary forms of action were inadequate. If we were right in thinking that the nomothete realized the advantages of his new procedure, we may reasonably believe that he applied it to a considerable number of offenses which had previously been punishable by one or another of the special forms of action. But such grave crimes as appeared from their very magnitude to call for the exercise of greater power and influence than the ordinary individual possessed evidently continued to be dealt with by the customary procedure.[28]

At this point it will be interesting to inquire what steps Solon the nomothete took against the particular abuses that had called forth vehement denunciations in the public utterances of Solon the citizen. Since our legislator was evidently not the sort of man whose memories or sensibilities are blunted by the acquisition of authority, we have a right to believe that they were not ignored. One of the crimes he denounces in the extant fragments,[29] the enslavement of poor citizens, had undoubtedly passed as a thoroughly legitimate and—in the minds of the wealthy—proper proceeding up to

[27] *Supra* 62 f.   [28] *Infra* 84 f.   [29] *Supra* 39.

this time; Solon, as we have seen, made it a statutory offense punishable by criminal action. The others, sedition, conspiracy, embezzlement of public or sacred funds, and the perversion of justice, must unquestionably have been looked upon as wrong and unlawful; probably all of them could be prosecuted by eisangelia in the council. There is no reason why Solon should not have extended the public action to offenses connected with the administration of justice and finance, with a view to more effective repression. Sedition and conspiracy, as we have seen, were probably not assimilated to the crimes punishable by public action. But it must be remembered that even these grave crimes were not left untouched; although the old forms continued to be followed, it seems that their administration was now entrusted to more democratic agencies. There is no reason to doubt Aristotle's assertion that Solon did not interfere with the judicial functions of the Areopagus.[30] But even if the powers this council formerly exercised over state offenders were not diminished or transferred to other bodies, a step had nevertheless been taken toward their more democratic administration, for the commons now participated in election of the magistrates from whom its membership was recruited.[31] And it is more than likely that these judicial prerogatives soon came to be shared, to some extent, by the new council of four hundred[32] or by the assembly. For we must not forget that they were not created or conferred by written laws or a written constitution, but constituted a jurisdiction founded upon ancient custom, very little of which could have been definitely prescribed in writing before the time of Solon. This being the case, the new council and the assembly would naturally undertake to exercise powers

[30] Ar. *Cons. Ath.* viii. 4; cf. Busolt II, 280 ff.   [31] Busolt II, 273–74.

[32] That Solon did establish a council of 400 is now generally regarded as beyond question, though a few historians still uphold the contrary opinion. For the controversy on the subject, cf. Busolt II, 279, n. 2, and, for a more recent statement of the argument against Aristotle's account, De Sanctis, 251.

that were not explicitly limited to the Areopagus but rather associated with the general functioning of a parliamentary body, the more as some of them apparently had been occasionally exercised by the assembly in earlier times.[33] The distribution of these functions among the three bodies, therefore, was probably never a matter of statutory prescription, but depended rather on political strength and efficiency, and from this time on we may expect to find the high jurisdiction over state offenders that once pertained almost exclusively to the Areopagus reposed largely in whatever body happens to be predominant at one time or another. This explains, among other things, how the Areopagus was able to regain so much of its former power in the period that followed the Persian wars.[34]

This is as far as we can go in the direction of positive reconstruction. But one significant limitation upon Solon's legislative activity is well established. It is very generally agreed that he made no attempt to modify that portion of the law, traditionally ascribed to Dracon, which regulated the prosecution and punishment of homicide.[35] In other words, he declined to include homicide in the category of crimes, and permitted it to remain a matter for action by the family, not the state. Whether he failed to recognize completely the criminal character of the offense, or hesitated to invade the precinct of religion and ancient ritual, we cannot say. Whatever may have been the causes of his inaction, it strengthens the impression already formed, that the Greeks were not nearly so concerned with the taking of human life as with other crimes that we look upon today as far less heinous.[36] Here we perceive once more that among the Hellenes the punishment of homicide, far from being "Das Centrum des Criminalrechts," and promoting the evolution of the ideas that led to the creation of criminal

[33] *Supra* 62. [35] Cf. Busolt II, 287; Glotz, *Solidarité*, 372; Gilbert, 140.
[34] *Infra* 100. [36] *Supra* 41 f.

law, is a thing apart from that evolution. The religious factor, which we are asked to look upon as the mainspring of progress in this direction, is again seen to retard, rather than accelerate, the normal rate of development.

Even this incipient attempt at reconstruction enables us to appraise Solon's contribution to the development of criminal law somewhat more precisely than has been possible in the past. It has been shown that some progress had been made in the punishment of crime before Solon. But the definition of crimes was based entirely upon custom, and was consequently vague; it expressed the interests, not of the whole body politic, but of the relatively small proportion comprehended in the privileged classes. Similarly, the customary criminal process which Solon found in existence had developed sporadically and unsystematically; it was readily available only to members of these privileged classes and applicable only to certain types of crimes. No one of the special forms was simple and flexible enough to be capable of universal application; no one of them could have been made the basis for a system of criminal procedure susceptible of indefinite expansion or adaptation to varying political conditions. Solon, having constituted the state along more democratic lines, accommodated its definition of crimes in some measure to its altered public opinion. But his great achievement was the introduction of the criminal process, modeled upon the old action in tort, later known as the graphe. The more immediate effects of this innovation were that the protection of the criminal law was extended to all citizens, while it became possible to punish crimes that had hitherto gone unpunished and easier to punish those that the state had already undertaken to repress. What is of immeasurably greater importance, however, to the student of political institutions, is that the introduction of this simple, effective, flexible process made it comparatively easy for the successors of Solon to evolve a rational and orderly system of statutory criminal law.

In all that has been sketched, the great nomothete was merely laying the foundations upon which succeeding generations of Athenians reared a noble edifice. It is his glory that he made them so true, and of so just a design, that the superstructure founded upon them, the invisible temple of Justice, had the exquisite proportion, the classic simplicity of outward adornment, the strength and symmetry, which have made its material counterpart, Athena's temple, the admiration of all time.

CHAPTER VII

CRIMINAL LAW IN ATHENS AFTER SOLON

Among the multifarious enactments traditionally attributed to Solon, those we have been able to pronounce unquestionably authentic seem pitifully few.[1] But, few as they are, they illustrate his handling of fundamental problems and give a fair idea of his larger policies; the light they cast upon the character of the man and the nature of his work is not to be despised. Solon evidently combined with the quickness and resolution that make for prompt and positive action the deeper qualities of mind that enable the statesman and philosopher to grasp the general bearings of his problems. His legislation, with all its limitations, was a tremendous advance upon the political arrangements characteristic of his age; as we look back, it seems almost incredible that in one year a single individual could have swept away so much of ancient usage and introduced so much that was to stand the test of time.

The aristocracy and
the laws of Solon

Having this impression, we should like to find that Solon's fellow-citizens evaluated his achievement somewhat as we do, that all factions generously accepted the results of his mediation in loyalty and unity of spirit. Unfortunately that is not the way of the world even today, nor was it then, as may be seen from Solon's own writings. Like all com-

---

[1] Linforth, 61 ff.; Busolt II, 258 ff.; Gilliard, 298 ff.; De Sanctis, 256 ff. Accounts naturally do not agree in all particulars; differences of opinion will be discussed in connection with the various institutions attributed to Solon.

promises, the Solonian constitution was unacceptable to those who held extreme views, whether conservative or radical.[2] It is superfluous here to repeat in detail the familiar story of the bitter factional struggles that led repeatedly to temporary interruptions of constitutional government, and finally after about thirty years to the tyranny of the Pisistratids; of the revolution that expelled the tyrants toward the close of the century and the welter of anarchy terminated by Clisthenes, who reconstituted the burgess body and reorganized the state upon new lines. What our inquiry seeks to trace in all this turmoil is the fate of Solon's criminal legislation. How much of it survived these intermittent paroxysms of anarchy and long periods of autocratic domination, either in practice or merely as a text of statutes long disused? And how much of what survived in one way or another was incorporated into fifth-century legislation?

First of all we must inquire whether it is likely that Solon's laws were actually repealed or materially altered in the course of the various aristocratic reactions and periods of anarchy that marked the next thirty years. The narrative of Aristotle, which is practically the only source for this period, would indicate that they were not, for it consistently gives the impression that the laws, although they were disregarded and overridden on more occasions than one, were not changed or repealed.[3] Furthermore, in summarizing these years of political unrest, Aristotle adduces as one of the underlying causes of the constant strife displeasure at the great change in political conditions brought about by the new constitution.[4] And in the account of the three parties which existed at the time of Pisistratus' first coup d'état, since the two extremist factions are virtually identical with the two groups of malcontents described by Solon him-

[2] Ar. *Cons. Ath.* xi and xii, with the quotations from Solon (=*frs.* iii, iv, xxx-xxxi, xxxii [Hiller-Cr.]).   Cf. Busolt II, 296.

[3] *Cons. Ath.* xiii.   [4] *Ibid.* xiii. 3.

self, it is evident that the "moderate policy" favored by the party of Megacles is the Solonian constitution.[5] Finally, although Aristotle was keenly interested in all constitutional changes, he says nothing of changes during this time, and the famous enumeration of the successive constitutions assigns the whole period to the constitution of Solon.[6] This shows clearly that Attic tradition knew nothing of any important formal modification in the Solonian legislation prior to the reign of Pisistratus.

It has generally been assumed without inquiry that this tradition is correct, and the text of Solon's laws remained practically untouched throughout these troublous times.[7] Yet a difficulty is involved which is far too serious to be ignored. How are we to explain the fact that the laws of Solon, though they were looked upon with dislike by the aristocratic factions,[8] and apparently set aside in practice when opportunity came, were not formally abrogated or revised? A careful inquiry into the actual conditions of the time may throw some light upon the problem. In the first place, it must be remembered that at this time written law was comparatively a new and unfamiliar thing, and, strictly speaking, the state possessed no permanent machinery for legislation. When it was judged necessary to enact or to revise a code of law, a special nomothete was appointed, as in the case of Solon, and invested usually with dictatorial powers.[9] And it is to be noted that the nomothete, far from

[5] This is established by *Cons. Ath.* xi-xiii (with the quotations), and is generally recognized (cf. Busolt II, 305, n. 2; Gilbert, 143, n. 1).

[6] *Cons. Ath.* xli. 2.

[7] Linforth, 93; De Sanctis, 259; Busolt, 290 ff.; Gilliard, 294.

[8] Linforth, 91 f.

[9] With familiar instances of early Greek lawgivers should be compared the traditional accounts of the decemviral legislation at Rome, which are now generally believed to approximate the facts (Goudy, "Roman Law," *Encyc. Brit.* XXIII, 538). The persistence of this tendency long after the appearance of permanent legislative machinery is attested by the extraordinary legislative commissions set up in the course of the oligarchic reactions that marked the close of the fifth century. For the history of legislative commissions in Athens, see the monograph of F. Smith, *Athenian Political Commissions* (Chicago, 1920). It must be remem-

expecting his laws to be changed or repealed and providing machinery for that purpose, usually made an attempt to render change difficult or impossible.[10] True statute law, flexible and responsive to varying conditions and sentiment, expressed through the medium of a permanent legislative department of government, was not to appear until much later. Hence at this time laws were far more likely to be simply overridden or disregarded than repealed or amended. It is probable that Solon did not expect his laws to be changed, and practically certain that he did not make any provision for their modification.[11] In the ordinary course of events they would remain, whether enforced or disregarded, until a political crisis of exceptional gravity led to the appointment of a nomothete or a special legislative commission.

In the second place, written laws were not then the formidable obstacle to political usurpation they later became, and it was easier and more natural to disregard them. To use for a moment the technical language of jurisprudence, the laws promulgated by Solon were not yet the commands of a sovereign authority; the two agencies which eventually gave the law of Athens that character, the assembly and the heliastic courts, were still in the weakness of infancy, a weakness which was gradually transformed into strength as

bered further that, even when legislative machinery was made a permanent part of government, it did not function continuously or independently of the assembly, but might be set in motion by a vote of the people, taken once each year in the assembly on the eleventh Hecatombaeon (Gilbert, 300 f.; Schoemann, *Gr. Alt.* I, 415 f.).

[10] This ancient feeling survived in the clauses so often found in later Athenian enactments forbidding repeal or amendment; its relation to legal fictions is brought out by Maine (chap. 2). Cf. the story told by Demosthenes (xxiv. 139–41) regarding the legislation of Zaleucus, which De Sanctis (258, n. 3) apparently takes in good faith as a provision for changes in the law.

[11] Here Grote, with his usual perspicacity, is well aware of what later historians are inclined to forget (III, 168 f.). It is immaterial whether we accept or reject the tradition that Solon bound the Athenians by oath to observe his laws for a term of years (cf. Linforth, 88); in this particular Solon must have been governed by the conceptions of his time, and not by conceptions whose development became possible only as a result of his reforms.

the numbers and power of the common citizens increased.[12] Nearly two centuries separate the era we are studying from the times when a successful coup d'état is followed promptly by abrogation of the laws and promulgation of a new code.

There were also more particular reasons why the aristocratic factions in power could well afford to disregard the existing criminal laws. The Areopagus and the magistrates remained undisturbed in the exercise of that broad criminal jurisdiction which was theirs by immemorial custom,[13] and the latter unquestionably could refuse to entertain criminal actions based on the statutes of Solon with but slight likelihood of being called to account.[14] Consequently, as long as the aristocratic factions controlled the council and executive offices,[15] they lacked neither means nor power to punish their opponents, and themselves had little to fear from the Solonian criminal action.

This very peculiar situation appears to result chiefly from Solon's failure to extend the franchise to the non-burgess population of Attica.[16] By his first sweeping reforms he had restored to citizenship those who had lost their status, and had evidently so strengthened the commons that the aristocratic party might well hesitate to abolish the heliaea or abrogate his laws.[17] But in declining to extend the franchise, he withheld that measure of power, later conferred by the reforms of Clisthenes, which enabled the commons to convert the assembly and the popular courts

[12] De Sanctis calls attention to the lack of centralized authority in Solon's scheme of government (258).

[13] Supra 61 ff.

[14] As I have elsewhere shown ("Athenian Magistrates and Special Pleas," Class. Phil. XIV, 338 ff.), even in the fourth century there was little limitation upon the magistrate's right to refuse a complaint.

[15] Although there were factions within the aristocratic party, it was unified in its opposition to the commons, and there cannot have been any real breach between the Areopagus and the annual magistrates until Pisistratus came into power.

[16] Cf. Busolt II, 274.

[17] Supra 54.

into effective political agencies.[18] Further, it must be remembered that the struggles of this period were primarily between aristocratic factions, and the faction temporarily in control probably never represented the total strength of the aristocratic element. At the same time, the necessity of reckoning with a non-citizen population of considerable numbers and wealth was still present, as in the time that preceded Solon's reform.[19] From all this it is easy to understand why the aristocratic party, though it looked with disfavor upon the Solonian legislation, never went so far as formal repeal. We may affirm with but little hesitation that, when Pisistratus became tyrant, he found the laws of Solon in existence if not actually in effect.

*Pisistratus and the
criminal acton*

Aristotle reports a well established tradition when he states that Pisistratus did not alter the existing laws but made them the basis of his administration.[20] Nor is this entirely incompatible with his later assertion that, when Clisthenes came into power, the legislation of Solon had "disappeared" by reason of disuse during the tyranny.[21] The first statement, which merely records the fact that Pisistratus did not abrogate existing legislation, cannot be taken to mean that he devoted himself to the meticulous enforcement of each and every law without regard to actual habit and practice. It would be equally absurd to infer from the second that in the time of Clisthenes the very text of all the laws of Solon had vanished utterly. When once the tyrant had established a *de facto* government, he was, like the

[18] There is much dispute as to precisely how far Clisthenes went in extending the franchise (cf. Busolt II, 409, n. 5), but it is generally agreed that he greatly increased the numbers and strength of the commons. The view that he did not grant the franchise to metics (Busolt, *loc. cit.*; De Sanctis, 337) not only contradicts the clear statement of Aristotle (*Pol.* 1275 b 36 f.; cf. *Cons. Ath.* xxi. 2, 4), but seems to me to be inherently improbable.

[19] *Supra* 52.   [20] *Cons. Ath.* xvi. 2, 8; cf. Hdt. i. 59; Thuc. vi. 54. 6.   [21] *Ibid.* xxii.1.

aristocratic factions, under no necessity of repealing the laws, since those not already long disused would be administered in his interest by officials he controlled. In fact formal repeal would have been positively detrimental to his interest, for it would have tended to alienate popular support. But after the laws had been administered for half a century by officials subservient to the tyrants, who could easily decline to enforce some ordinances while stressing others, they must have come to embody above all else the will and interest of the ruling family. The legislation found actually in effect by Clisthenes certainly could not be thought of as Solon's, no matter what proportion of it was actually his work.[22] Attempts have been made occasionally to distinguish what of Solon's legislation must have been discarded and what retained, but the attention directed toward criminal law and process has been negligible. Yet here if anywhere the little we know concerning the general sequence of political events seems to offer a basis for credible conclusions.

Pisistratus, once in control of the state, relying upon his armed force and upon some measure of popular support, apparently lost no time in introducing his friends and adherents into the chief annual magistracies.[23] But the Areopagus, composed of ex-magistrates belonging almost without exception to the hostile aristocratic factions, could not be so easily or speedily revamped.[24] During the earlier

[22] There must have been occasional legislation during the régime of the Pisistratids, though we have no means of determining its form (resolutions of the assembly, or perhaps official edicts); it is difficult to see how the circuit judges could have been instituted, or a new system of taxation established, without the promulgation of an ordinance of some sort.

[23] This was the practice of the Pisistratids, consistently throughout the entire period of their régime (Thuc. vi. 54. 6–7). When the tyranny was first established and not yet securely entrenched (cf. Ar. Cons. Ath. xiv. 3), the necessity of controlling the chief offices must have been particularly cogent.

[24] It is very unlikely, in the light of the statements cited in n. 20, that Pisistratus attempted any revolutionary measures in dealing with the Areopagus. Nor have we reason to believe that the power of the Areopagus was seriously affected by flight or banishment of members in the early years of the tyranny (cf. infra 97).

years of his ascendancy it must have been the principal organ of opposition to his designs, and a formidable one, possessed as it was of a far-reaching criminal jurisdiction created, not by laws that might be repealed, but by ancient custom.[25] How was the new ruler to combat it? One might reply that he could have assailed its members before the assembly or council, as did Ephialtes later,[26] and procured the enactment of laws curtailing its powers. But there is no reason to believe that at this time, before he had won the support of the masses by various measures subsequently introduced for their relief,[27] he had full assurance of a majority either in the council of four hundred or in the assembly. It must be remembered that the men whose confiscated wealth later provided him with means to gratify the commons were probably for the most part members of the body he was fighting and still far from defeated.[28] Furthermore, it may well be that he was reluctant to destroy or reduce to weakness an institution he could eventually make exceedingly useful. In these circumstances, the alternative to a conflict of which the issue might be uncertain was to strengthen the annual magistracies, already held by his supporters, as a counterweight to the influence of the Areopagus. But the executive and judicial powers attached to these offices under the aristocracy must have depended to a very considerable extent upon the cooperation of the Areopagus; the archon facing a hostile Areopagus was undoubtedly much less of a force in the state than was the archon with its support. In particular, while it is unlikely

[25] *Supra* 84. [26] *Infra* 100 ff. [27] Ar. *Cons. Ath.* xvi, especially 2 and 9.

[28] It is clear from accounts of the first expulsion (Ar. *Cons. Ath.* xiv. 3; Hdt. i. 60) that few of the aristocratic leaders had been exiled at that time. Ure (*The Origin of Tyranny* [Cambridge, 1922], 35 f.) believes that Pisistratus was a "mining promoter" and built up his "third party" by judicious distribution of financial assistance. Whatever may have been the original source of his wealth, we have in Aristotle a reasonable and entirely credible account of steadily increasing popularity and financial strength; both are sufficiently explained by his policy of encouraging the agricultural operations of the small landowner (Ar. *Cons. Ath.* xiv) and favoring commercial enterprise. See Bury, 194 ff.

that the defection of the magistrates could immediately effect a serious diminution of the judicial powers exercised by the Areopagus over state offenders, the prestige and power of the magistrates may well have been materially affected by the separation. Be that as it may, Pisistratus was certainly under the immediate necessity of strengthening the officials in every practicable way, and making their jurisdiction in criminal cases as broad and authoritative as possible; nothing that tended to the accomplishment of this design could be overlooked. Among the courses open to him it would be difficult to find any that would be more effective in securing this result or would more readily suggest itself than the rehabilitation of the public action. This form of process, as we have seen, though it contained vast possibilities, had probably not been allowed to develop to any great extent under the aristocratic régime.[29]   The results for which Pisistratus could hope from its employment were both immediate and sustained. He could prosecute his political enemies before magistrates friendly to his interest, instead of the hostile Areopagus or bodies not yet fully committed to his cause, and in so doing could effectively increase the power and prestige of these magistrates. There is no period to which the first real attempt to develop the possibilities of Solon's criminal action can be more credibly assigned than the earlier years of the tyranny.

This is rather strikingly borne out, in my opinion, by the institution of the circuit judges.[30]   Briefly stated, the inter-

[29] *Supra* 92.

[30] Ar. *Cons. Ath.* xvi. 5. Cf. Busolt II, 330; Lipsius, *Recht*, 32. De Sanctis flatly rejects Aristotle's statement that Pisistratus established the circuit judges (313). His principal argument, that "Pisistrato avendo diviso l'Attica non in demi ma in naucrarie, is suoi dicasti rurali avrebbero dovuto prendere il loro nome da queste," is valueless, since we know that the demes, though first utilized for administrative purposes by Clisthenes apparently, are the ancient rural hamlets of Attica (cf. Gilbert, 147, n. 1), and κατὰ δήμους may mean little more than κατ' ἀγρούς. The other argument, that in the nature of things the thesmothetes could not have been too busy in the time of Pisistratus to attend "alle cause rurali," is sheer assumption, and like many such assumptions fails to take into account the actual political situation.

relations are these. The superior magistracies were the only organs of government of which the usurper could quickly acquire control; the only effective weapon he could readily employ against the Areopagus and his individual opponents was the criminal action, which the legislation of Solon had assigned to those magistrates and chiefly, it would appear, to the thesmothetes. When we find Pisistratus creating a new civil jurisdiction, we are tempted to conclude that he wished to relieve the superior magistrates of pressure put upon them by the increasing frequency of public actions, and, by transferring the bulk of civil litigation to other officers, to utilize all their energies in the attack upon the Areopagus.[31] And when we find this same jurisdiction re-created in the fifth century, by opponents of the Areopagus, under very similar conditions and for the precise purpose here suggested, the conclusion seems inescapable.

During the last years of Pisistratus' life and the reign of Hippias, the circumstances that had tended to emphasize the importance of the criminal action were materially altered. Every year had seen the induction into the Areopagus of former magistrates who were adherents of the tyranny; at the same time natural causes conjoined with extensive proscriptions[32] were steadily diminishing the representation of the hostile aristocratic factions that once had dominated the body. There can be little doubt that, by the time the tyrants were expelled, the Areopagus had come to be a willing

[31] The considerations stated by Aristotle (xvi. 3–5) no doubt entered into the motives which led Pisistratus to establish the court, but they are not alone sufficient to account for the institution. It was unquestionably to the tyrant's advantage to have a prosperous rural population, intent upon the cultivation of its lands. But if we are to believe that the new court was instituted merely to keep the peasants from coming to town, we must go further and accept the naïve tale preserved in Pollux (VII, 68), that the Pisistratids caused the peasants to wear a coarse garb so they would be ashamed to show themselves in town. The story smacks of the later feeling toward tyrants.

[32] After the battle at Pallene, the chief opponents of the Pisistratids seem either to have gone into exile or to have been banished or even put to death (Hdt. i. 64). On the extensive proscriptions during later years of the tyranny, cf. And. ii. 26; Isoc. xii. 148; xvi. 25–26; Ar. Cons. Ath. xix. 1.

tool in the execution of their behests.   Invested by ancient
custom with ample judicial powers, unfettered by the limitations of written law and definite procedure, it became,
when once entirely subservient to the ruling family, a peculiarly effective instrument for disposing of enemies under the
forms of law.[33]   With such a weapon ready to hand, the
tyrants were no longer under the necessity of emphasizing
and strengthening the ordinary criminal action or the
criminal jurisdictions of the annual magistrates.   This does
not, of course, justify the assumption that any great proportion of the criminal law fell immediately into disuse, since it
was clearly the policy of the Pisistratids to afford the ordinary citizen adequate legal protection against crime as well
as civil wrongs.[34]   But it does show that the development of
criminal law which may be believed to have marked the earlier
years of the tyranny must soon have abated very materially,
and that some of Solon's criminal enactments may well have
been among the laws which fell gradually into disuse.

Clisthenes

Like Pisistratus, Clisthenes found his political opponents
entrenched in the Areopagus.[35]   But, unlike Pisistratus, he
stood at the head of a powerful and apparently united
popular party.[36]   He could count upon the support of the

[33] We do not know unfortunately whether the heliaea ever functioned under the
Pisistratids, or whether appeals were ever taken from the judgment of a magistrate.
In any event the tyrants would prefer a tribunal whose procedure was unfettered
by written law, from whose decisions appeal was in those times absolutely
unthinkable.

[34] This is clear from the whole tenor of ancient accounts of the Pisistratids.

[35] Those members of the old aristocratic factions who had not joined the
Alcmaeonids seem to have affiliated themselves gradually with the tyrants (cf.
And. ii. 26).   This explains the difficulties discussed by Busolt (II, 401, n. 2,
with studies cited).   Hence we find the majority party of the aristocratic element
headed by Isagoras, "a friend of the tyrants" (Ar. *Cons. Ath.* xx. 1).   By the end
of the Pisistratidean régime the Areopagus was made up entirely of men who
held office under the patronage of the tyrants.

[36] As a result of the economic and agrarian policies of the Pisistratids, the
commons were now in a very different position from that in which they found
themselves after Solon's reform.

assembly, which his initial reforms had made actually the repository of sovereign power, and of his council of five hundred, which was virtually a committee of the assembly.[37] Furthermore, the numbers and power of the Areopagus had unquestionably been greatly diminished by wholesale banishment or proscription.[38] Consequently he had not the same motives for developing the possibilities of the criminal action. The institution of ostracism would seem to indicate that it was his policy to rely upon a direct judgment of the people in dealing with political opponents, and this is borne out by the few instances of important political trials known to us from the early part of the fifth century, which seem invariably to have taken place in the assembly.[39] Furthermore, among the measures traditionally ascribed to Clisthenes there is none which points to any particular interest in criminal legislation. It would appear that the time and energy of the lawgiver were completely absorbed in procuring the enactment of his far-reaching constitutional changes, and that he found in the customary judicial powers of parliamentary bodies, especially the assembly, adequate means of dealing with powerful opponents.

On the other hand, it would be a mistake to overlook the indirect effect upon the criminal law and its administration of those measures which Clisthenes enacted with broader purposes. It is generally agreed that he was responsible for the first really effective organization of the popular courts, which led to constant exercise of the privilege of appeal and ultimately reduced the judiciary to the position of examining magistrates.[40] This of course completely changed the character of the criminal courts. Again, in establishing the assembly as the sovereign power in the state, Clisthenes

---

[37] On the Clisthenian council, cf. Ar. *Cons. Ath.* xxi. 3; Busolt II, 430 ff.

[38] Herodotus states that the Athenians who joined Isagoras and Cleomenes in seizing the Acropolis were put to death (v. 72). Modern historians are disposed to regard this as a mistake, and hold that they withdrew from Attica with Cleomenes under safe-conduct (Ar. *Cons. Ath.* xx. 3; cf. Busolt II, 405, n. 1).

[39] Cf. Lipsius, *Recht*, 179 ff.   [40] *Ibid.* 32 ff.

paved the way for the introduction of permanent legislative machinery which was to become an inexhaustible source of statute law, both civil and criminal.   His contribution to the development of criminal law and procedure is therefore none the less important from being in a measure incidental to larger designs.   He probably did not seek to augment or subject to revision those criminal enactments of Solon whose texts had survived the disorders of factional strife and the tyranny.   Nor can we believe that he made any particular effort to revive such of them as may have fallen into disuse. But without the fundamental changes he introduced into the legislative and judicial departments of government, the tremendous expansion which the criminal law was soon to undergo would have been impossible.

The reforms of Ephialtes

The next and unquestionably the greatest stage in the growth of criminal law falls toward the middle of the fifth century.   Again, as in the time of Pisistratus, the causes are to be found in the circumstances of a struggle against the Areopagus, the famous contest which resulted in the reforms of Ephialtes and Pericles.   And again, while the general relationship between this struggle and the strengthening of the popular courts is matter of common knowledge, its particular and intimate connection with the development of criminal law has been generally overlooked.

During a time just subsequent to the Persian wars, according to Aristotle, the Areopagus gradually usurped many important functions of state and exercised extensive powers, of which it was deprived in 462 by the reforms of Ephialtes.[41]   In the redistribution of these powers among

---

[41] *Cons. Ath.* xxiii-xxv.   Cf. De Sanctis, 399 ff.   To just what extent Aristotle exaggerates the influence of the Areopagus in this period is immaterial.   That it exercised great powers is certain; I have elsewhere observed that such a usurpation of powers conferred by unwritten custom was a natural, in fact almost inevitable, concomitant of political ascendancy.   (*Supra* 84 f.)

the various departments of government, judicial functions which the Areopagus had arrogated to itself were conferred upon the courts.[42] Here again, as in the case of Solon's institution of the criminal action, the change which Aristotle describes in a few words is not so simple as it seems, and what historians are accustomed to speak of as "a law" must in reality have involved somewhat far-reaching and complicated legislation. What the Areopagus was not to do, could no doubt have been set forth easily in a single resolution; but it was not so simple to define with sufficient precision what the courts were to do, to prescribe how various magistrates were to handle numerous cases that had previously found their way into the Areopagus.

As contrasted with the council of five hundred and the assembly, the Areopagus was strongly conservative; it naturally became the focal point of opposition to the pronounced democratic and imperialistic trend of the times.[43] Among the powers and prerogatives it had preserved or temporarily recovered, not the least formidable was that ancient and broad criminal jurisdiction which had enabled it to ignore the criminal action of Solon.[44] Having in this a means of assailing democracy in its most vital part by appropriating the functions of the popular courts, it found an opportunity in the failure of the popular officials to cope with the situation created by the Persian invasion of Attica. Revival of its former prestige enabled it to regain at least a considerable portion of these extensive powers, which, as has been pointed out, were based on ancient usage rather than written law.

When Ephialtes and his associates found themselves sufficiently strong to take these powers from the Areopagus and confer them upon the courts, their immediate and pressing problem was to create for those courts jurisdictions

---

[42] *Ibid.* xxv. 2. [43] Cf. Busolt III, 261–62; De Sanctis, 399. [44] *Supra* 92.

secure against encroachment. Necessarily close attention had to be directed toward procedure, as well as substantive law. The Areopagus had apparently ignored jurisdictions set up by existing laws, and had also found in such processes as eisangelia means of exercising indeterminate powers of punishment in the case of offenses for which statutory provision had not been made. Consequently it must have been imperative to scrutinize the adjective provisions contained in existing laws and in some cases to make them more precise, and also to enact new statutes defining and expanding the criminal jurisdictions of the various magistrates. It is reasonable to believe that most of the new actions were assigned to the court in which they lie in the fourth century, that of the thesmothetes.[45]   What is of greatest importance from our point of view has generally not been perceived, the judicial reform that took place at this time was first and foremost a reform of criminal law and procedure, and pre-eminently of the criminal law that later was administered by the thesmothetes.

This sudden expansion of the criminal law is attested by the creation in 453 B.C. of a new—or rather the revival of an old—civil jurisdiction, the circuit judges.[46] The real significance of this step, which has apparently escaped students of Attic law and, with one exception, historians as well, we are now in a position to comprehend.[47]   The

[45] Cf. Lipsius, *Recht*, 374 ff.

[46] Ar. *Cons. Ath.* xxvi. 3; cf. *supra* 96.

[47] So far as I can discover, only De Sanctis (136, 444) has glimpsed the causes underlying the institution of this new civil jurisdiction.   Gilbert is quite wrong in concluding that the purpose was "merely to relieve the Heliast courts from the business of deciding unimportant cases" (157).   Cases involving trifling claims had never been decided by the heliastic courts, and were merely taken from the thesmothetes and entrusted to the circuit judges; cases involving larger claims continued to be sent to the dicasts by the circuit judges precisely as they had been by the thesmothetes; the first attempt to relieve the pressure upon the dicastic courts of which we hear was the institution of the public arbitrators, and this was much later (cf. Bonner, "The Institution of Athenian Arbitrators," *Class. Phil.* XI (1916), 191–95).   My reasons for believing that the circuit judges were first instituted by Pisistratus have been given (*supra* 97).

increasing burdens thrown upon the superior magistrates by expansion and systematization of the criminal law fell most heavily upon the thesmothetes; these magistrates already handled the bulk of civil litigation, it would appear, and were charged with the general administration of a court system which was becoming every day more active and complex. Some measure of relief became imperative, and the problem was solved by instituting the court of the circuit judges, and perhaps other civil jurisdictions,[48] to which most of the private actions of the thesmothetes were transferred. This would make for the prompt and effective handling of civil cases and at the same time leave the higher magistrates free to devote their energies mainly to public actions. It is at least significant that the establishment of the circuit judges is merely a revival of the institution devised by Pisistratus when he was obliged to cope with similar problems.

The creation of this new court of exclusively civil jurisdiction must inevitably have resulted in greater attention to private law and its administration. Thus the judicial reform which began with changes in the criminal law, desirable from political considerations, made necessary one adjustment after another until the whole system of justice had been revised, extended, and strengthened. There can be little doubt that during the ten or fifteen years following 462 both branches of Attic law, with the judicial organization required for their administration, were fully perfected in every essential respect.[49] By the middle of the fifth century, approximately, the criminal law of Athens had attained its maturity. Although it was subjected to revi-

---

[48] The introduction of the εἰσαγωγεῖς and the ναυτοδίκαι is ascribed to this same general period (De Sanctis, 444; Lipsius, *Recht*, 84 ff.). These new courts are of course partly accounted for by the judicial activity consequent upon the growth and centralization of the Athenian empire. But this does not explain the striking circumstance that at this time it was found necessary to relieve the thesmothetes of practically their entire civil jurisdiction.

[49] Cf. Lipsius, *Recht*, 37.

sion on at least two occasions toward the close of the century, there is nothing to indicate that it was materially altered or augmented.[50]

Antiquity of the graphe

Having completed the historical portion of our study, we may return for a moment to the interesting, though relatively unimportant, problem of the time at which the graphe, the written notation of criminal actions by magistrates or their deputies, was first introduced.   In a previous study I pointed out that γραφή was a familiar term for criminal actions as distinguished from civil suits in 425 B.C.[51]   It can now be said definitely that the introduction of the graphe, inasmuch as it preceded the major development of criminal law, cannot be dated later than the reform of Ephialtes.[52]   In fact one is tempted to regard it as part of that reform, since a thoroughgoing reorganization of criminal jurisdictions, with particular attention to procedure, unquestionably presented a favorable opportunity for such a change.   This attractive solution is however open to a very grave objection.   The written notation of private actions, as well as public, was also a familiar, well established practice in 424/3,[53] and, if the graphe was first introduced only some thirty-five or forty years earlier, it is difficult to

[50] The notable revisions of the law followed the overthrow of the Four Hundred and of the Thirty.   In each instance, although unquestionably changes were introduced, the primary aim of the revision was the restoration of democratic institutions after a period of revolution and disorganization, and the law probably was not fundamentally altered or largely supplemented.   This is well brought out by Smith in his careful study of the earlier revision (*Pol. Com.* 71, n. 29; 73 ff.). On the revision under Euclides, cf. Bury, 588 f.   Evidence is accumulating in support of my suggestion of an important judicial reform in 378/7 ("Oral and Written Pleading," *Trans. Am. Phil. Assoc.* L, 193); Glotz has discovered from a study of inscriptions ("L'épistate des proèdres," *Rev. Ét. Gr.* XXXIV (1921), 1–19) that the change of presiding officers in the assembly was made in this year.   However there is nothing to indicate material changes in the substantive law.

[51] "Oral and Written Pleading in Athenian Courts," *Trans. Am. Phil. Assoc.* L (1919), 180.

[52] *Supra* 58, 100 ff.   [53] "Oral and Written Pleading," 180 f.

understand how there was time for the word γραφή to develop the specialized sense of "criminal action." This use of the term, as I have already observed, attests a considerable time during which only public actions were noted in writing.[54] Furthermore, since the notation of private actions was an established practice as early as 424/3, we need scarcely hesitate to ascribe its introduction to the reorganization of civil jurisdictions and procedure consequent upon the reestablishment of the circuit judges in 452.[55] If this be correct, the introduction of the graphe in criminal process must be credited to Clisthenes, Solon, or possibly Pisistratus.

What little is known regarding the use of writing in Athens in these early times is entirely compatible with the belief that Solon himself introduced the graphe and this was the original form of his new criminal action. Written laws attributed to Dracon had been in existence for a quarter of a century, and there had probably been some writing down of laws in a much earlier time.[56] Solon tells in his poems of the tablets set to record mortgages on land; these were apparently to be seen in great numbers on every hand, and we cannot conceive how they could have served their purpose had they not borne inscriptions, as in later times.[57] It would be quite absurd to maintain that the written notation of actions by officials could not have been practiced at this time, when writing was so extensively used to record transactions between private individuals.

[54] *Ibid.*, 178.   [55] *Supra* 103.

[56] Aristotle states that the thesmothetes were first appointed in order that they might record and preserve τὰ θέσμια (*Cons. Ath.* iii. 4). I am not entirely in accord with the view that the thesmothetes did no more than record decisions (Lipsius, *Recht,* 12, n. 44; cf. Ziehen,"Die drakontische Gesetzgebung," *N. Rhein. Mus.* LIV (1899), 335 ff.), which depends principally on a passage now generally admitted to be an interpolation (*Cons. Ath.* xli. 2: μετὰ δὲ ταύτην ἡ ἐπὶ Δράκοντος, ἐν ᾗ καὶ νόμους ἀνέγραψαν πρῶτον). See Busolt II, 172 ff. It is however, immaterial for our present purpose whether θέσμια are judgments, customary law, or even the materials of a rudimentary code; it is the fact of a written official record with which we have to do.

[57] *Fr.* xxxii (Hiller-Cr.). 6: ὅρους ἀνεῖλον πολλαχῇ πεπηγότας. On the ὅροι in later times, see Lipsius, *Recht,* 692 ff.; abundant examples may be found in any collection of Greek inscriptions.

While there would seem to be no reason for refusing to regard Solon as the originator of this written notation, it would perhaps be unwise, without more conclusive evidence, to affirm positively that he was. It is entirely possible that his new criminal procedure, like the more ancient special forms of action,[58] was oral, and that the graphe was devised by Pisistratus in reviving the criminal action.[59] There is less probability that the innovation should be credited to Clisthenes, since his reforms appear to have been mainly constitutional.[60] On the whole, I am disposed to regard it as most probable that the written notation of actions was devised by Solon as a feature of his new criminal process, and was extended to civil suits when the civil jurisdiction of the circuit judges was reestablished.

[58] *Supra* 63.   [59] *Supra* 96.   [60] *Supra* 99.

CHAPTER VIII

CRIMINAL LAW IN OTHER STATES OF HELLAS

In tracing the several stages through which the criminal law of Attica passed in the course of its history, we get distinctly the impression that the Athenian legislators were inventors and originators, striking out new lines of progress and not merely copying or adapting the practices of others. It is not only that the general direction of legal evolution in Athens was determined by social and political forces inseparable from the steady trend toward democracy. Specific steps are found in almost every instance to result from combinations of circumstances not likely to have been duplicated elsewhere; they aim at the solution of problems which must have pressed upon Athenian statesmen with peculiar urgency. And it is a priori likely that here as in so many other fields, Athens took the lead. Such considerations as these, however, do not justify the assumption that Solon and his successors learned nothing from the practices and theories of others. Athens was constantly in contact with states whose legal and political institutions were looked upon by many of her leading men as greatly superior to her own, and she cannot have remained ignorant of the significant strides that were being taken in the Hellenic cities of the West. Before our task is finished, we must seek to discover what others were doing toward the perfection of criminal law and its adaptation to changing conditions of civic life. There is unfortunately little evidence, and that little comes chiefly from a time when the process we have been tracing was complete. Only in the case of Crete and

Sparta will it be possible to essay anything like a reconstruction even of general outlines; elsewhere we must be content to glean here and there a scattered hint toward the solution of our problem.

Crete

A study of Cretan institutions is of especial importance in our inquiry by reason of the high esteem in which they were held by the proponents of aristocracy,[1] and because here we are in a position to check the passing allusions of ancient writers against more copious and ancient epigraphical material than is usually available.   In addition to the famous inscription from Gortyna, we have a large number of fragments from various Cretan sites, and can trace with some confidence the general outline of the constitution.[2] Unfortunately for our purpose, the inscription from Gortyna, although it presents certain departments of the law in minute detail, is concerned chiefly with matters of a civil character, and yields little or no information on many points that are vital to our inquiry.   It does, however, show the stage of legal development the Cretans had attained in the fifth century, and in one or two instances treats specifically of offenses that we now regard as crimes.

The legal and political institutions of the Cretans in the fifth century, so far as they are known to us, present striking analogies with the pre-Solonian state in Attica.[3]   The government is purely aristocratic.   At the head of the state are the board of magistrates known as cosmi, chosen from

---

[1] Cf. Plato *Laws* 631B; *Rep.* 544C.

[2] The most complete collection of these sources is probably that of Comparetti, *Le leggi di Gortyna e le altre iscrizioni arcaiche Cretesi* (*Monumenti antichi* III, Milan, 1893).   References here are to the text published with translation and commentary in *Recueil* I, 352 ff.

[3] *Supra* 43 ff.   It would seem from the few instances in which comparison is possible, and from the tendency of ancient writers to speak of "Cretan institutions," that the law of Gortyna may safely be regarded as typically Cretan.   Cf. *Recueil* I, 489.

certain privileged kinship groups, and a council of elders made up, like the council of the Areopagus, of former magistrates.[4] The general assembly of the citizens appears to exercise very little power, meeting merely to ratify the decisions of the cosmi and council.[5] Even in the time of Aristotle, the Cretan cities were notorious for turbulent strife and anarchy resulting from the incessant rivalry of aristocratic factions.[6] Judicial arrangements are such as would naturally be expected in a political organization of this type.[7] (There is no trace of popular courts, and decisions of judges are final.) Slavery for debt is recognized and protected by law as well as custom, though measures have been taken to secure certain rights to enslaved debtors.[8] The use of witnesses seems to be chiefly formal,[9] and the evidentiary oath is constantly prescribed by law.[10]

A portion of the inscription deals with the penalties for adultery, rape, and criminal assault. These offenses are treated as torts, not crimes; they create a right of action on the part of the victim, parent, or relative, for the recovery of pecuniary damages in amounts determined by the character of the offense, the status of the parties, and sometimes other circumstances.[11] It is almost inconceivable that there could have been a public action for adultery in Gortyna at a

[4] Ar. Pol 1272 a 26 ff.; cf. Recueil I, 416 ff.

[5] Ibid. 1272 a 10 ff.; cf. Recueil I, 417.

[6] Ibid. 1272 b 7 ff.

[7] For detailed and careful studies of the judicial machinery and procedure, see Smith, Hesiod to Solon, chaps. 3 and 5; Recueil I, 729 ff.; Koehler and Ziebarth, Das Stadtrecht von Gortyn and seine Beziehungen zum gemeingriechischen Rechte (Göttingen, 1912), 80 ff., 125 ff.

[8] Cf. the "second code" (RIJG xviii), col. vi., with the commentary (p. 488).

[9] Cf. Recueil I, 432 f. and Headlam, "The Procedure of the Gortynian Inscription," Jour. Hell. St. XIII (1892–93), 51 ff. Headlam's view, that the witnesses are without exception 'formal' is not accepted by the editors of the Recueil (loc. cit.).

[10] The instances, including compurgation, are cited and discussed by Smith, Hesiod to Solon, chap. 5; cf. also Recueil I, 433 ff., and Koehler and Ziebarth, 82 ff.

[11] RIJG xvii, col. ii, lines 2–45. For an analysis of the elaborate system of tariffs, which suggest the early Germanic law, cf. Recueil 419, 451 ff.

time when these extremely archaic provisions—"un débris de l'époque archaique," as they have been aptly termed— were publicly inscribed.[12]

In the detailed regulations regarding the marriage and guardianship of "heiresses" we find no provision for the protection of their rights by public action, such as the Attic law contained at an early time. The right of action appears to be vested exclusively in the relatives.[13]

The nearest approach to the principle of public action in our inscription is a provision relating to cases in which an individual is claimed as a slave. Anyone who may be present when a man is being seized without judgment of court is authorized to offer him asylum.[14] This is the only instance I have been able to find in the entire document which appears to contemplate action by others than those whose rights have been invaded. Another notable clause among the rules applying to these cases explicitly establishes a legal presumption of freedom.[15] Furthermore, it has been credibly inferred that the penalty exacted for holding a free man as a slave went to the person who intervened in his behalf and upheld his freedom before the court, the intention of the legislator being to encourage intervention by the prospect of a reward.[16] Even if we do not accept this view, the two provisions just cited are sufficient to show that the primitive law of tort was revealing its inadequacy and under-

---

[12] A public action at Gortyna against adulterers taken in flagrante delicto is described by Aelian Var. Hist. xii, 12. The editors of the Recueil assume that his statement refers to the time of the Gortynian inscription, and cite instances in which damages are supplemented by a fine (451, especially n. 4). I am inclined to believe that the statement of Aelian, if it is to be credited, should be referred to a much later period. However, it must be remembered that even after the introduction of the γραφὴ μοιχείας in Attic law, extremely primitive and fantastic modes of private vengeance were sanctioned in Athens; cf. Recht, 429 ff.

[13] Thus a right of action against other claimants vests in the heir-at-law (RIJG xvii, col. viii, lines 53 ff.), against the heir-at-law, for failure to perform his obligations, in the relatives (τὸς καδεστάνς) of the heiress (ibid. col. vii, lines 40 ff.).

[14] RIJG xvii, col. xi, lines 24 f.; cf. p. 446, and Buck, Introduction to the Study of the Greek Dialects (Boston, 1910), 275.

[15] Ibid. col. i, lines 14 ff.; cf. p. 447.

[16] Recueil I, 446.

going modification in consequence of the very problems that had confronted Solon a century and a half earlier in Attica.[17] It is to be regretted that we have no information regarding the punishment of homicide or of offenses that directly affect the commonwealth. It is probable, however, that at this time the Cretans dealt with homicide in accordance with the same fundamental principles that are seen in the Attic law; these seem to have been very generally disseminated among the Hellenes, perhaps as a result of Delphian influence.[18] As regards attacks upon the state, the council and chief magistrates no doubt exercised a traditional criminal jurisdiction developed from those archaic processes to which we have traced the special forms of criminal action in Attic law.[19] What had not yet been achieved, apparently, was the application of the simple procedure of the old action in tort to the punishment of crime. Even in the fifth century, it would seem, the Cretans had not yet devised or borrowed from others a form of criminal action comparable to the graphe. Furthermore, if we may judge from their treatment of rape, adultery, and similar offenses, they were still unaware that many attacks upon individuals are in reality attacks upon the community.

In the matter of penalties the action in tort exhibits here and there a slight tendency toward a quasi-criminal character. In general the penalty enforced for an attack upon an individual goes to the plaintiff by way of damages or compensation, but in a few instances a fine, payable to the state, has been added to or substituted for the purely civil remedy.[20] Confiscation of property is the punishment incurred by the judge who fails to decide certain cases within

---

[17] *Supra* 78 ff.   Cf. the Roman practice of requiring a smaller sacramentum from the *adsertor libertatis* (Strachan-Davidson I, 60); on the procedure in Roman law, cf. *Dict. Ant.* IV, 623 (s.v. *praejudicium*).

[18] Isoc. iv. 40; cf. *Recht*, 619.   On the influence of the Delphic oracle, cf. *Recht*, 14.   See also Treston, 154 ff.

[19] *Supra* 59 ff.

[20] Cf. *Recueil* I, 436 f., 486, 493; Koehler and Ziebarth, 79 f.

the time prescribed.[21]   Disfranchisement is probably to be included in the list of punishments, though it could apparently result from a civil process, seizure for debt.[22]   Both punishments are almost certain to be employed by a society in the stage of legal development represented by the Gortynian law, but we cannot say whether they could be inflicted as the result of an action in tort or were reserved for the grave crimes that were presumably dealt with by the council or the cosmi.

Sparta

Spartan institutions, like those of Crete, were regarded with intense admiration by the proponents of aristocratic or oligarchic government, especially by practical politicians, who found in the commanding position attained by Sparta a weighty argument in favor of their views.   To this admiration we are indebted for much of our information regarding the Laconian state; since it was directed primarily to other departments of their political system than the judicial, our knowledge of their legal institutions in the fifth and fourth centuries is unfortunately vague and unsatisfactory.

(The council of elders exercised judicial powers very similar to those vested in the Athenian Council of the Areopagus in the sixth century and earlier;[23] it tried all cases of homicide and of high crimes and misdemeanors against the state, and was the only tribunal that could inflict the death penalty upon a citizen.[24]   The five ephors, who were the political heads of the state during the greater part of the fifth and fourth centuries, heard and decided

[21] *RIJG.* xix B; cf. p. 435.

[22] The fact of disfranchisement may be inferred from *RIJG* xvii, *col.* ix, lines 31 ff.; as the editors note, the loss of the franchise resulted from seizure or mortgaging of the person for debt; cf. pp. 416, 487 f.

[23] *Supra* 84 f.

[24] Busolt I, 550 ff., especially 552; Gilbert, 80; Kahrstedt, *Griechisches Staatsrecht* I (Göttingen, 1922), 249.

practically all civil suits, and their decisions were final. They also received and brought before the council for trial accusations charging grave offenses against the state, and in addition exercised a summary police jurisdiction of tremendous scope, embracing probably all cases in which the dealth penalty was not inflicted.[25] Those inferior magistrates charged with enforcement of the numerous regulations by which every detail of the citizen's life was ordered necessarily took cognizance of offenses coming within their respective departments, but probably brought all cases before the ephors and were accountable to them for their official acts.[26] The kings still acted as judges in cases involving family matters and were charged with the enforcement of certain laws touching the public highways.[27]

Here again we have in general outline the traditional judicial arrangements of the Hellenic peoples, substantially as they existed in Attica before Solon and in Crete down to a much later time.[28] An extensive criminal jurisdiction, which apparently has its origin in the primitive forms of action studied in an earlier chapter, is shared by the ancient council of elders and its chief executive officers. These officers, the principal magistrates of the state, decide all civil cases, and from their decisions there is no appeal. Unfortunately we have practically no information which would enable us to say definitely just what matters the Spartans classed as civil and what as criminal. It is quite evident that the criminal jurisdiction of the council and the ephors, like that of the Areopagus and the Athenian magistrates,

[25] Busolt, 555 ff., especially 564; Gilbert, 81. Kahrstedt believes they could even inflict the death penalty (238).

[26] How numerous and detailed were these regulations is apparent from Xenophon's treatise On the Spartan Constitution, or Plutarch's Life of Lycurgus, not to mention the information scattered through the pages of the historians and the other works of Plutarch. On the relation of the inferior magistrates to the ephors, cf. Busolt, 564; Gilbert, 59; Kahrstedt, 219, 237 ff.

[27] Hdt. vi. 57; cf. Busolt, 548; Gilbert, 81; Kahrstedt, 227.

[28] Supra 52 f., 109.

was limited to grave offenses against the state, and perhaps
heinous crimes, and did not extend to ordinary attacks upon
individuals; for protection against these, the citizen clearly
depended upon the civil jurisdiction of the ephors, in other
words, upon the old action in tort. And it is equally
apparent that the processes involved in the punishment of
grave offenses could not have been readily available to the
ordinary citizen, who did not enjoy the advantages conferred
by influence or official position. We can have little doubt
as to the stage that has been attained in the evolution of
criminal law; there has as yet been no fusion between the
primitive law of tort and the archaic processes by which
crimes are punished.

From a somewhat different point of view, however, the
law of Sparta presents a strange anomaly. As has been
said, the life of the citizens was regulated in minute detail
by a great mass of ancient customary law, strictly enforced
by magistrates with ample powers of punishment.[29]   Any
violation of these rules, even the most trivial, was evidently
regarded as an offense against the state. Not only was it
the duty of the magistrates charged with their enforcement
to proceed against offenders, but we may be sure that any
citizen was permitted and expected to denounce violations.
Here then we have a body of law, undoubtedly much more
voluminous than the criminal statutes of such a state as
Athens, which will meet the test of any purely formal definition of criminal law. By what criterion do we pass it by
and say that Spartan law has not, despite its peculiar
development in these directions, attained a position in
advance of the Attic criminal law? The answer is not a
simple one.

The solution of the difficulty is to recall the characteristics proposed at the commencement of our inquiry as
essential to true criminal law.[30]   This particular body of

[29] *Supra* 113.   [30] *Supra* 5.

law, despite its volume and the minute detail of its regulations, is not complete; it does not involve, apparently, full recognition of the principle that attacks upon individuals may be violations of the public peace and good order, nor does it make adequate provision for the protection of the rights annexed to the persons or property of individuals.

Furthermore, it should be pointed out that this type of process finds its true analogy, not in the criminal jurisdiction of the dicastic courts in Athens, but in the police powers given to various magistrates to punish offenses of a trivial character without reference to a dicastic court.[31] This summary jurisdiction of the magistrates in Athens was a survival from the more extensive powers they exercised before the system of dicastic courts was fully perfected, and the transfer of all but the most trivial offenses to the jurisdiction of the popular tribunals, which tended to the separation of executive and judicial functions, was the real advance. This Spartan body of law did not lose its primitive character by the mere process of extending and multiplying the powers of punishment vested in public officials.   Such criminal law as this, often voluminous and detailed, is found in barbarous or semi-barbarous societies.

The fundamental difference which these characteristics of Attic and of Spartan law suggest is in fact a difference in the material aims of the law.   Furthermore, it is a difference which is invariably found when a mature, rational system of law is compared with the legal notions and practices of communities in a less advanced state of political organization.   The aim and final purpose of the Attic law was justice, regarded not merely as a means toward a more harmonious and effective political organization, but also as an end, desirable in and for itself.   Thus the Attic law proceeded by establishing and defining the rights and duties of individuals toward one another and toward the state, by

[31] Lipsius, *Recht*, 53.

seeking to reconcile and adjust where there might be conflict, and by setting up adequate processes for the protection and enforcement of rights attaching to individuals as well as those pertaining to the state. Few would deny that it is this conception which made the Attic and the Roman law preeminent among ancient systems known to us. This is a distinctive characteristic of modern European legal institutions, including of course our own, and this it is alone which can justify the claim of jurisprudence to be regarded as an independent science and not merely a department of politics.

On the other hand, it is clear, even from the few facts we have been able to adduce regarding Spartan legal institutions, that Sparta had not attained to this conception of the law. The additions which Sparta has made to the primitive Hellenic "common law" have not this broad and lofty intent. The justice toward which they look is not so much an end per se as a means, and the ultimate aim of these minute regulations and their strict enforcement appears to be the creation and preservation of a state which shall achieve its greatest efficiency in war. Even this aim was at times secondary to another, the retention of power in the Spartan oligarchy.

Here we are face to face with the most obvious deficiency of the purely formal definitions advanced by jurists of the analytical school, disregard of the material aims of the law.[32] Were our criterion merely a formal definition, we might be tempted to conclude that Sparta had made greater strides than Athens toward the perfection of criminal law. By the same process of reasoning one might be led to overestimate the importance in legal history of the voluminous and detailed ordinances by which an autocratic chieftain sometimes seeks to secure his power, or the countless taboos promulgated by the priest-rulers of a barbarous tribe.

[32] Cf. Vinogradoff I, 118 f.

It must not be thought that the attention to justice of which we have been speaking affords a test by which all legal systems can be segregated into two classes, those which exhibit it and those which do not. It is of course present in some degree in all political societies, from the most primitive to the most advanced, and we proceed from one extreme to the other by insensible gradations. But among those peoples who have achieved the most in the perfection of law, it has directed and informed the whole process of legal development. Without it the Athenians would never have learned to distinguish so clearly between those rights which the individual may be trusted to enforce for himself, and those which must be protected by the state.

In conclusion, we may observe that the criminal process of Sparta, unlike the Attic, distinctly tended to be inquisitorial, rather than litigious.

The cities
of the West

After Crete and Sparta, our thoughts turn naturally to the Hellenic states of Sicily and southern Italy; it was here, if we accept the prevailing opinion of antiquity, that forensic eloquence had its origin and law was first enacted in writing. But we cannot believe that either Zaleucus or Charondas made any notable advance on the side of criminal law. Aristotle states explicitly that the one and only contribution of Charondas to legal progress was his institution of the action for perjury,[33] and we are the more inclined to accept his judgment when we recall the emphasis he else-

---

[33] *Pol.* 1274 b 5 ff. There can be little question that the action was civil; in Attic law even in the fourth century perjury could be prosecuted only by the individual directly affected (Lipsius, *Recht,* 778 ff.). The only provision for public prosecution of perjury that has come to my notice is found in a Delphian inscription of the third century (Haussoullier, *Traité entre Delphes et Pellana* [Paris, 1917], 70 ff.). Although the Aristotelian authorship of the passage from the *Politics* has been questioned (cf. Haussoullier, 175 ff.), the substantial correctness of the statement regarding Charondas is generally admitted.

where puts upon Solon's introduction of the criminal action.[34]
And the assertion of Demosthenes,[35] that the law of the
Locrians has gone practically unchanged for more than two
centuries, even though we cannot regard it as literally true,
would indicate that the legislation of Zaleucus ushered in a
period of conservatism, not progress.   Furthermore, even if
we accept unhesitatingly as the authentic work of the two
famous nomothetes every measure credited to them by
ancient writers, we find nothing comparable in importance
to the criminal legislation of Solon.[36]   So far as can be
judged from the scant and dubious record the western lawgivers have left behind, they followed the ancient Hellenic
tradition in their definition and punishment of crimes and
continued to treat attacks upon individuals as torts.   The
particular enactments for which they are given credit may
appropriately be considered in connection with similar rules
of law in other states.

Other Hellenic
states

Despite the progress made during recent years in the
recovery of inscriptions, the materials for a study of criminal
law and procedure in the fifth and fourth centuries, except
for the states already discussed, are hopelessly inadequate.
Consequently, it will be well to arrange the little we have
with reference to types of offenses or forms of process.   This
method will enable us to examine as a whole the traditional
"common law" of the Hellenes, in so far as it has to do with
the punishment of offenses.   Although it is not my intention to include the Hellenistic period, documents from that
age must receive attention when they appear to justify

[34] *Cons. Ath.* ix. 1; cf. *supra* 56.

[35] xxiv. 139 ff.

[36] For a general summary of the measures attributed to the western lawgivers,
cf. Smith, "Early Greek Codes," *Class. Phil.* XVII (1922), 187 ff.; Koehler and
Ziebarth, 89 ff.

inferences in regard to the practice of an earlier time.[37] It will be sufficient here to cite typical instances illustrative of general tendencies; a detailed account of the treatment of particular offenses is more appropriate to a systematic exposition of substantive criminal law.

The offenses which appear to have been very generally defined and punished as crimes in the various states of Hellas fall under the following heads: (1) treason, including attempts at tyranny, betrayal to an enemy, and sedition;[38] (2) attempts of individuals or magistrates to obstruct the operation of a law or decree, or to procure its abrogation or repeal in violation of an express prohibition;[39] (3) the refusal or failure on the part of a private individual to comply with a law or decree embodying a policy or obligation assumed by the state as a whole;[40] (4) the refusal or failure of a magistrate entrusted with the enforcement of a law or decree to carry out its provisions;[41] (5) trespass or encroachment upon a public or sacred domain;[42] (6) the violation of sumptuary laws or regulations having to do with good morals.[43] It is manifestly unwise to press the argument from silence when our epigraphical material is still so fragmentary, yet we

[37] For example, offenses treated as torts in Hellenistic times are not likely to have been matter for criminal prosecution in the earlier period, and archaic forms of process prescribed in Hellenistic legislation may generally be assumed to have been employed in the classical era. However, each problem must be considered by itself; the general principle of criticism involved I have elsewhere attempted to formulate (*Class. Phil.* XI [1916], 365, n. 2).

[38] Instances are cited *supra* 68, n. 41.

[39] E.g., *RIJG* ix. 29 ff., 53 ff., 56 ff.; i. 32 ff.; xiB. 13 ff.; cf. *RIJG* xiii *bis* (= *CIA* II. 1055), where the resolution of a deme is in question, and the threat of civil prosecution takes the place of a state penalty.

[40] E.g., *RIJG* ix. 43; *CIA* IV. i. 27a, lines 32 ff.

[41] E.g., *RIJG* xiB. 18 ff.; decree of Amorgus (*Ath. Mitt.* I [1876], 343; cf. *BCH* XVI [1892], 276 ff.), lines 50 ff.; *RIJG* xixB. 6 ff.

[42] In the famous inscription from Heraclea (*RIJG* xii) trespassers are ejected by state prosecution, but there is no reference to penalty (*infra* 123, n. 61); in a mutilated Athenian decree of Roman times (Εφ. Αρχ. 3d series, II [1884], 167–70), future sales of certain sacred lands are punishable by γραφὴ ἀσεβείας (line 9)

[43] E.g., *RIJG* ii and iii; the editors of the *Recueil* cite many examples and analogies (I, 12 ff.). On the matter of process and penalties, cf. *infra* 121 ff.

cannot fail to observe the absence of enactments defining
and punishing as crimes attacks upon individuals.[44]

The texts just cited yield some interesting information
with respect to penalties and procedure. In a few instances
the legislator apparently relies entirely upon the religious
sanction in the matter of punishment, and makes no reference to the secular authority of the state;[45] here unquestionably we have primitive survival, suggesting the conviction noted in Hesiod that the gods will intervene to punish
crime.[46] The ancient formulae which pronounce outlawry
upon the offender, and often upon his descendants as well,
with confiscation of goods, are found frequently in connection with offenses of the first three classes, particularly the
first, as we have had occasion to note.[47] Occasionally the
religious sanction is invoked along with outlawry, and in
provisions for confiscation the property is not infrequently
dedicated, entirely or in part, to some deity.[48] In a number
of instances violators of the law are to be prosecuted by
eisangelia, usually introduced by a magistrate;[49] in others
phasis is prescribed, and a reward offered as an encouragement to individuals to initiate prosecutions.[50] In the enactments which have to do with the dereliction of magistrates,
we find in many instances that a penalty is prescribed,

[44] An exhaustive search may, of course, discover enactments of this sort, but
I should be inclined, upon the basis of the material I have studied, to regard them
as exceptional.

[45] A good example is the famous inscription from Teos (CIG 3044=Michel,
1318); others are collected by Schoemann, Gr. Alt. II, 272, and Ziebarth, "Der
Fluch im griechischen Recht," Hermes XXX (1895), 57 ff., where the subject is
fully discussed with abundant references. The fact that the present enactment
provides no penalty other than the imprecation does not of course imply that
offenders could not be punished by the state.

[46] Supra 34.

[47] E.g., CIA IV. 27a (=Michel, 70), lines 34 ff.; CIA I. 31 (=Michel, 72),
lines 20 ff.; CIA II. 17 (=Michel, 86), lines 51 ff.; Michel, 1335, lines 40 ff.; RIJG
i. 32 ff.; ix. 32 ff., 56 ff.; xiB. 13 ff. Cf. also RIJG xxii, passim, and the passages
cited supra 68, n. 41 (tyranny).

[48] This is the case in several inscriptions cited in the preceding note.

[49] CIA IV. 27b, lines 58 ff.; cf. Michel, 263A, lines 21 ff.

[50] Cf. CIA II. 17 (=Michel, 86), lines 41 ff.

usually a fine, but nothing is said regarding procedure;[51] in other instances, however, the technical term εὐθύνειν ("to correct," usually associated in Attic law with the examination of an official's conduct at the close of his term of office) is used, in the passive voice, with the genitive of the penalty (e.g., εὐθυνέσθω, εὐθυνέσθων).[52] It would appear that the process against magistrates commonly associated with the first functioning of the heliaea in Athens and supposed to have been introduced by Solon was usual in such cases; where the procedure is not specified, we may credibly infer some sort of denunciation, such as eisangelia or endeixis, in council or assembly.

Sumptuary laws

From the point of view of criminal law, enactments falling under the general head of sumptuary legislation have many features of interest.[53] The extant examples obviously embody comparatively ancient usage. Usually the offenses dealt with are not of the types that immediately and directly threaten the common welfare or the security of the state. Nor do they as a rule constitute invasions of rights annexed to individuals. As a class they resemble the acts which are "technically criminal" in modern law, statutory misdemeanors, *contraventions*, rather than *crimes de droit commun*.[54]

[51] E.g., *RIJG* xxii. IV (=Michel, 524D), lines 5 ff.; *CIA* II. 11 (=Michel, 6), lines 19 ff.; *CIA* IV (I). 35c (=Hicks, 58), lines 20 ff.; *CIA* I. 9, lines 11 ff., 18 ff. In a good many instances there are hints from which we can make some inference as to the procedure contemplated, and at times we find a definite prescription, as in Hicks, 93, lines 26 ff.; Michel, 8, lines 6 ff.; *CIA* IV (I). 35c (=Hicks, 58), lines 11 ff. (if we accept the usual restoration πρυτάνης in line 13). So far I have not found any striking departures from the familiar forms of criminal procedure.

[52] E.g., *CIA* IV. 53a (=Michel, 77), lines 9 ff., 18 ff.; *CIA* I. 40 (=Michel, 74), lines 37 ff.; *CIA* IV. 27b (=Michel, 71), lines 18 ff. Cf. the allusion to εὔθυναι in *CIA* IV. 27a (=Michel, 70), lines 70 ff.

[53] The best examples are *RIJG* ii and iii, enactments regulating burials and rites in honor of the dead. For other laws of similar character, attributed to various nomothetes, see the commentary to *RIJG* ii.

[54] See Stephen, *Hist. Crim. Law* III, 263 ff.; Craies in *Encyc. Brit.* VII, 454, *s.v.* "criminal law."

Consequently the origins of such enactments, although they must go back to a fairly ancient time, cannot be closely connected either with the primitive law of tort or with archaic methods of punishing crimes against the community. They represent rather an early extension of the criminal jurisdiction of the state to include acts which affect the state, not immediately or patently, but indirectly and in a secondary degree; moreover, their presence in the statutory enactments of the Hellenic cities implies a more conscious and thoroughgoing analysis of the duties and obligations of the individual toward the state, and a more complex conception of what constitutes public welfare, than we should expect to find in the earlier stages of political development. Their wide dissemination and substantial similarity, however, bespeak great antiquity, and much of their content no doubt goes back to early family law and custom; we may perhaps find their prototypes in such archaic conventions as governed the conduct of women in Homeric times.[55] Inasmuch as violations of sumptuary enactments seldom affected the rights of individuals, enforcement must have depended from the first upon some form of public prosecution. This task was sometimes entrusted to special officials, who were authorized no doubt to inflict summary punishment for petty offenses and to refer graver violations to a court.[56] Where there were no such officials, the right of prosecution must have been thrown open to all citizens, as in the case of other offenses with which the state concerned itself.

[55] Ancient writers had the habit of attributing these measures, like other early enactments, to famous nomothetes, and especially to Solon (cf. *Recueil* I, 12 ff.). It is more reasonable, however, to conclude that Solon and the other early legislators were systematizing and codifying, perhaps with considerable modification, the ancient custom of the Hellenic peoples.

[56] In Gambreum in the third century the enforcement of the law was entrusted to the γυναικονόμος (*RIJG* iii. 17 ff.). This office, which seems to have been a common one in the Greek states, was identified in the mind of Aristotle with the aristocratic forms of government (*Pol.* 1300 a 4 ff.); the evidence for its existence in Athens is late (Gilbert, *Cons. Ath.* 160, n. 3).

Two inscriptions
from Heraclea

An extremely interesting case of prosecution by officials is found in the famous Heraclean inscriptions of the fourth century regarding the sacred domains of Dionysus and Athene Polias.[57] Commissioners have been appointed at a special session of the assembly to survey the precincts of these deities, to recover such portions as may have been unlawfully appropriated by private individuals, and to subdivide and let the lands as determined by the survey.[58] The reports of the commissions give a detailed account of their operations and include, in the case of the first inscription, the text of the contracts with the new tenants.[59] Where the "squatters" refused to vacate, the commissioners filed thirty-day actions and recovered the sacred lands by judgment of court.[60] There is no allusion to a penalty, and the object of the proceedings seems to be merely recovery;[61] what interests us is the legal action taken by the state through the commissioners. The future supervision of the new lease contracts is entrusted to the "city commissioners" ($\pi o\lambda\iota a\nu\acute{o}\mu o\iota$).[62] If the lessees fail to plant trees and vines to a prescribed number, they are liable to heavy fines; apparently the official report of the city commissioners, with a special board of not fewer than ten citizens, is to be taken as proof of the facts, and the commissioners will proceed to execution as if upon a judgment of court.[63] By other penal clauses of the contract the lessees are made liable for certain acts under existing laws and forms of action; if they cut or damage trees, or excavate, or quarry, except as provided in the

[57] *RIJG* xii, tables I and II; the following references, unless otherwise specified, are to the lines of table I.

[58] 8 ff.   [59] 94–186.   [60] 48 ff.

[61] This was equitable, since many of the boundary marks had been obliterated (e.g., 56 ff.), evidently as the result of long neglect, and it would be difficult to establish an intention to trespass upon the domain.

[62] 104 ff., 110 ff., 117 ff., etc.   [63] 122 ff.

agreement, or permit others to do so, they are liable to prosecution for damage to sacred domains;[64] if they mortgage their holdings or give them in pledge, they are liable to prosecution "as provided by law."[65]   Since the city commissioners are not mentioned in these clauses, we may conclude that some form of action open to any citizen is contemplated; unfortunately we know too little of Heraclean institutions to attempt any conjecture as to the procedure, though it is a priori probable that some one of the traditional forms would be employed.   It is interesting to note that omissions usually lead to the imposition of fines by the city commissioners; the performance of certain forbidden acts will be matter for prosecution under existing law.   From this it is clear that the Heracleans had defined as crimes sundry acts relating to sacred lands in general; the particular duties enjoined upon the lessees of this domain are made a part of the contract.   Fines imposed by the commissioners for such omissions, if not paid by the lessees, fall upon their sureties, who are responsible in their persons and their property, without further legal action, for any and all obligations of the lessees.[66]   If the city commissioners fail to enforce these provisions, they are themselves responsible (ὑπόλογοι) according to the terms of the contract;[67] unless the ephors were charged with the enforcement of this clause, we must conclude that some form of process similar to those just described was employed.   Certain offenses, apparently of minor importance, are punishable with fines imposed by the commissioners, without a court trial.[68]   The lessees are expressly given a right of civil action against any who may trespass upon the domain, and are encouraged to seek the heaviest damages they can recover;[69] the trespass is treated as an invasion of private rights, but the ultimate interest of the state is kept in mind.   From other inscriptions which

[64] 135 ff.   [66] 154 ff.   [68] E.g., 133 ff.
[65] 149 ff.   [67] 178 ff.   [69] 128 ff.

treat of the leasing of sacred lands we are led to conclude that the provisions contained in our text are fairly typical of general Hellenic practice in the fifth and fourth centuries.[70]

*A general
comparison*

One might go on almost indefinitely, noting here and there in inscriptions matters that fall within the scope of our subject, fines and other penalties, summary police jurisdiction of magistrates, sporadic instances of criminal actions and state prosecution, and international agreements touching certain crimes.[71]   A complete and detailed study of these legal phenomena, however, can best be made in connection with a systematic study of substantive criminal law; for our present purpose, which is to get some idea of the general trend of development and to assign to Attic law its proper place, the examples that have been given will suffice. Obviously, with so few data before us, sweeping generalizations must be avoided and dogmatic insistence is quite out of place.   But even this brief survey would seem to justify the formulation of certain conclusions, if for no other reason, in order that their validity may be tested by further examination of the evidence.

We get distinctly the impression that in general, Athens had gone much farther than other Greek states in elaborating and reorganizing the traditional criminal law of Hellas and in perfecting machinery for its application.   In most states the tendency to separate judicial functions and to set up officials with purely judicial powers and responsibilities seems to have operated chiefly in the realm of civil law;[72]

[70] The more important inscriptions on this subject are cited in the commentary (*Recueil* I, 224 ff.).

[71] E.g., the agreement between Mytilene and Phocaea touching the responsibility of officials entrusted with the coinage (Michel, 8); cf. also Michel, 1.

[72] In Gortyna, for example, the dicasts seem to have been practically the only officials whose functions were purely judicial, and their jurisdiction was apparently limited to civil cases (*Recueil*, I, 430); it is probable that the arbitrators were private individuals; in any event arbitrations seem to have had no connection with criminal cases.

the application of criminal law continued, apparently to the end of the classical period, to rest with officials whose duties were mainly executive and with bodies that were primarily legislative.[73] In Athens, on the other hand, the application of criminal law was at a very early time centralized in the thesmothetes, whose functions were principally judicial;[74] even in the fifth century weighty criminal cases, originating in denunciations before the council or assembly, were frequently sent to a dicastic court for trial, and by the middle of the fourth century trials by the assembly were a thing of the past.[75]

The Athenians seem to have made equally great strides in the development of the substantive criminal law, and in this respect, as well as in their courts and their procedure, to have been appreciably in advance of their neighbors. This opinion is not founded solely upon the precarious argument from silence, but is supported by instances in which an actual comparison is possible. For example, in decrees giving to aliens the status of proxeni or public benefactors, most states gave no more definite assurance of protection to the recipients of the honor than was contained in the somewhat vague grant of σωτηρία.[76] Athenian decrees of this type generally contain a clause charging certain specified officials with the duty of protecting the individual named from any wrong at the hands of another;[77] in other words a wrong against one of these privileged persons is made a crime and matter for state prosecution. The contrast bespeaks not merely closer attention in Athens than elsewhere to the formulation of law, but also a relatively advanced conception of those duties and powers of the state which are normally embodied in its criminal law.

[73] Cf. what has been said in regard to the handling of criminal cases in Gortyna and in Sparta, supra 111, 112 ff.

[74] Supra 97, 102; cf. Lipsius, Recht, 11 f.　[75] Lipsius, Recht, 182, 205 ff.

[76] E.g., Michel, 189, 191, 192, 197, 203, 204, 207 ff.; 218 ff.

[77] E.g., Michel, 79, lines 15 ff.: καὶ ὅπως ἂν μὴ ἀδικῆται ἐπιμέλεσθαι τήν τε βολὴν τὴν ἀεὶ βουλεύοσαν καὶ τοὺς στρατηγὸς καὶ τὸν ἄρχοντα τὸν ἐν Σκιάθωι ὃς ἂν ἦι ἑκάστοτε. Cf. ibid. 73, lines 2 ff., 91, lines 15 ff., 99, lines 5 ff., 102, lines 29 ff., etc.

In our study of the process by which the criminal law of Athens was brought to the state of completeness and maturity it attained in the fifth century, we came to the conclusion that the introduction of the graphe was a factor of tremendous importance and that the graphe was devised by Athenian legislators.[78]   In support of this opinion, we may note that in Ilium, as late as the third century, the terms δίκη and δικάσασθαι are still officially used of criminal prosecutions, despite the fact that complaints in criminal cases are in writing.[79]

In general, I think we may conclude that the process by which the criminal law of Athens was evolved was in its essentials original and independent, and that the achievements of the Athenians in this direction were not equaled by any other Greek state in the classical age.

[78] *Supra* 86, 107.
[79] Michel, 524B, lines 37, 46, C, lines 5, 10, and especially D, lines 36 ff.

CHAPTER IX

CONCLUSION

In conclusion, an attempt may be made to summarize briefly certain fundamental characteristics of the Attic law as it was administered during the last century or so of Athenian independence. This will round out our understanding of the evolutionary processes we have been attempting to trace, and will give some indication of the direction further study of the subject might well take, namely, a systematic reconstruction of the substantive criminal law.

The maturity of Attic law is associated in the mind of the student with the fourth century before Christ. This results rather from our fuller knowledge of that period than from differences between the law of the fifth and of the fourth century, or from any great superiority observed in the latter. Attention naturally is focused upon a period which is thrown into bold relief by the speeches of great forensic orators, the writings of historians and political philosophers, and a wealth of inscriptional material. But it must not be forgot that the maturity of the Attic criminal law, as regards both its general character and completeness, probably goes back to the middle of the fifth century.[1] During somewhat more than a hundred years preceding the battle of Chaeronea it exhibits the same unity of spirit and of form that is observed in the literature of Athens from Aeschylus to Demosthenes; and the classical period of Athenian letters is likewise the classical period of Attic law.

[1] *Supra* 103.

Consequently, a systematic exposition of the perfected criminal law would properly include the data from this whole time, attempting more precise determinations only when they are material to the purpose in hand or of especial historical interest.

Criminal and
quasi-criminal actions

A rational system of criminal law implies a definition of crime. At the commencement of our inquiry we had to do with times in which the conception of "crime" was but faintly foreshadowed in the attitude of society toward certain acts and still scarcely differentiated from the broader and more elementary conception of "wrong" or "injury." Consequently we took as a starting point a very general definition of crime —a wrong that affects the political community as a whole.[2] In attempting to determine what acts were so regarded we found a criterion in the processes by which various wrongs were dealt with, and concluded that offenses which the entire community undertook to punish were looked upon as crimes, while those that were left to the particular individual or group directly affected were regarded rather as torts or private wrongs. If this criterion be applied to the mature Attic law, wrongs (acts or omissions) punishable by public actions (graphe and the various special forms) may be classified as crimes, and that part of the law which is enforced by means of public actions as criminal law.[3] But the matter is not quite so simple in the classical period as this might indicate. In the course of time the conception of crime has become more complex, and the machinery for the punishment of crime more complicated.

[2] *Supra* 1 ff.

[3] *Supra* 13; cf. Lipsius, *Recht*, 238 ff. Although Lipsius regards this as the essential characteristic of the graphe, it must be remembered that he does not identify the graphe unreservedly with the criminal action; for a criticism of this point of view, cf. *supra* 10, 13.

While the vesting of the right of action in the body politic is undoubtedly the essential characteristic of the public action, there are almost invariably other differences.[4] The prosecutor, when he has once initiated a criminal action, is not free to abandon or to settle it out of court, as in civil proceedings. Court fees are paid only by the prosecutor and are retained by the state. In case of conviction the court imposes a penalty to be exacted by the state, instead of giving judgment for damages or compensation to be collected by the plaintiff; the penalties ordinarily imposed include death, exile, total or partial loss of civic rights, confiscation of property, and fine.[5] From these characteristics of the criminal action, it would appear that for the definition of crime just proposed (an act or omission punishable by public action) we might substitute almost any of the definitions found in modern penal codes and treatises on law. It would be in substantial accord with the principles of Attic criminal law to describe a crime as a wrong whose sanction is punitive and may be enforced or remitted only at the discretion of the state;[6] or as an act or omission in respect of which legal punishment may be inflicted;[7] or as "an act or omission forbidden by law and punishable upon conviction by death; or imprisonment; or fine; or removal from office; or disqualification to hold or enjoy any office of trust, honor, or profit under the state; or other penal discipline."[8]

While the great majority of actions in Attic law are easily discriminated as criminal or civil according to the presence or absence of these distinguishing characteristics,

---

[4] The principal differences between the graphe and the civil action are discussed by Lipsius, *Recht*, 243 ff. Cf. also Heffter, *Die athenäische Gerichtsverfassung* (Cologne, 1822), 111 ff.

[5] Lipsius, *Recht*, 930 ff.; Thonissen, 91 ff.

[6] Cf. Kenny, *Outlines of Criminal Law* (Cambridge, 1904), 15.

[7] Stephen, *Hist. Crim. Law*, I, 1.

[8] *New York Penal Law* (Gilbert's *Criminal Law and Practice of the State of New York* [Albany, 1921], 2). Imprisonment, as a punishment, was unusual in Athens.

there is an intermediate group made up of actions which present some of them but not all. Perhaps the most conspicuous of these are the various actions relating to homicide, which are exceptions to the principle of public prosecution and differ in other respects from the public action, but lead to severe penalties in case of conviction.[9] The δίκη ἐξούλης, an action against a judgment debtor who resisted execution, is distinguished from ordinary private suits by the fact that it led concurrently to civil redress and a punitive fine.[10] Again perjury before a court was matter for civil action, but a third offense entailed the loss of civil rights.[11] Such actions as these may be regarded as quasi-criminal, and we should expect to find the criminal nature of the acts with which they had to do only imperfectly recognized in Attic law.[12]

*Sovereignty and the
sources of criminal law*

The distinction familiar to students of Anglo-American law between crimes at common law and statutory crimes apparently has no parallel in the fourth century, when the source of criminal law was almost exclusively legislative enactment. Originally, of course, the only source of criminal law was unwritten custom, and it is impossible to say even approximately how much of this ancient custom had been embodied in written rules prior to the time of Solon, either by the thesmothetes or by Dracon.[13] So far as we can discover, statutory enactments first become important as a source of true criminal law with the legislation of Solon

[9] Lipsius, *Recht*, 600 ff.

[10] Lipsius, *Recht*, 664 ff. This is the case also in regard to the δίκη βιαίων and the δίκη ἐξαιρέσεως (cf. Lipsius, *Recht*, 245, n. 18).

[11] Cf. my "'Επίσκηψις and the δίκη ψευδομαρτυρίων," *Class. Phil.* XI (1916), 386, where further citations will be found.

[12] Heffter, 114.

[13] The laws attributed to Dracon perhaps took cognizance of some of the offenses punishable under the customary law by ἀπαγωγή, ἐφήγησις, etc., but probably not of the graver offenses over which the council had jurisdiction (cf. *supra* 84 f.).

and the institution of the criminal action. In the fifth century they tended to supplant all other sources, and in 403 it was expressly enacted that henceforth no criminal prosecution was to be based upon an "unwritten law."[14] This statute, to judge from its wording, seems to have applied primarily to the criminal jurisdictions of the several magistrates and there were some few exceptions. High crimes and misdemeanors not explicitly forbidden by law could still be prosecuted by eisangelia,[15] and such ancient customs as were preserved by the Eumolpidae seem to have been taken into account in the punishment of certain offenses of a religious character.[16] But the sources of criminal law in the fourth century were in general (1) statutes regularly enacted, (2) resolutions of the assembly, in so far as they did not conflict with any statutory provision, and probably (3) resolutions of the council, within the limits of its jurisdiction as defined by statute.[17]

Closely related to the sources of the law is the subject of sovereignty. The development of the Roman law cannot well be understood without some knowledge of the doctrine of the *imperium* and the practice of vesting it in individuals. Nor can a history of English criminal law afford to neglect the prerogatives of the crown. In the same way, before undertaking an analysis of the criminal law of Athens, it will be well to review briefly the process by which that sovereign power to which alone appertains the right and duty of punishing crime came at last to be embodied solely in the assembly. Under the pre-Solonian régime, the

---

[14] And. i. 85 ff., especially 89: ἀγράφῳ δὲ νόμῳ τὰς ἀρχὰς μὴ χρῆσθαι μηδὲ περὶ ἑνός.

[15] *Supra* 62; cf. Lipsius, *Recht*, 184 f.

[16] Lipsius, *Recht*, 359, n. 6; cf. Vinogradoff II, 75 ff.

[17] Cf. Gilbert, *Cons. Ant.*, 277. The resolution of the council mentioned in [Dem.] xlvii. 33 ff. probably contained a sanctioning clause; otherwise the power given to trierarchs to seize equipment (33) would mean nothing. The law quoted and commented on in And. i. 87–89 (cf. Dem. xxiii. 87) also indicates that resolutions of the council sometimes contained penal clauses.

sovereign power in the state was unquestionably reposed in the aristocratic council, later known as the Council of the Areopagus.[18] The temporary delegation of certain powers to annual executive officers never developed into anything comparable to the grant of the *imperium* in Rome, though it might have done so but for certain of Solon's measures. When Solon instituted the right of appeal from judgments of the magistrates to the heliaea and transferred to the assembly the power of electing magistrates, he vested in the assembly, at least by the letter of the law, the final sovereignty in elections and in the administration of justice.[19] This sovereignty was realized in actual practice after the reforms of Clisthenes when the assembly acquired a real preponderance of power,[20] and it was extended to the enactment of law as a natural corollary to its administration.[21] It would be a mistake, however, to believe that this transfer was an immediate consequence of Clisthenes' reforms. The Areopagus naturally retained a considerable part of its ancient sovereignty, not explicitly vested in the assembly. This included, as we have seen, the important criminal jurisdiction based upon custom, which tended to be shared by the new council of five hundred.[22] It was only gradually that these remnants of sovereignty were taken from the two councils and appropriated to the assembly one after another by legislative enactment. One and the same process sub-stituted legislation for other sources of the law and conferred

---

[18] *Supra* 44.   [19] *Supra* 56, 84.   [20] *Supra* 99.

[21] It is interesting from the point of view of historical jurisprudence to note that in Athens judicial functions seem regularly to have preceded legislative. The ancient customary law was apparently administered for centuries before it came to be formally enacted in writing. As has been observed (*supra* 91), Solon apparently made no explicit provision for future legislative action when he was drawing up his laws and establishing an appeal to popular courts; the enactment of general legislation by the assembly seems to have assumed importance only after the popular courts were well established. However, resolutions on special subjects, such as the decree of Aristion authorizing the bodyguard of Pisistratus (Ar. *Cons. Ath.* xiv. 1) were no doubt passed by both assembly and council from very early times.

[22] *Supra* 84 f.

upon the assembly the sovereignty of the state. How the exercise of the judicial functions attaching to this sovereignty was entrusted by the assembly to various organs of government belongs to the study of criminal jurisdictions and procedure.

Athenian classification
of crimes

The Attic law, like other systems, failed to develop a general technical term for crime that included all wrongs punished by criminal action as distinguished from those that were matters for civil suit.[23]   Nor does it exhibit a classification of crimes according to the severity of the penalties involved; there is nothing comparable to the peculiar distinction in Anglo-American law between felonies and misdemeanors or the more logical discrimination found in Continental codes between *crime* and *delit*, *reato* and *delitto*, *Verbrechen* and *Vergehen*. The trivial offenses, however, that correspond in general to "summary offenses," *contraventions*, *contravenzioni*, were sharply set off from more serious crimes in point of procedure and penalty, though they did not receive any distinctive appellation.[24]

This inattention to the classification of crimes on a basis of comparative gravity appears to result mainly from the character of the Athenian penal legislation, in which procedure, jurisdiction, and consequences of conviction were separately and specifically provided in each statute;[25] there were apparently very few, if any, general rules whose enforcement was inseparable from insistence upon general definitions, such, for example, as the common law rule that

[23] *Supra* 75, n. 7.

[24] In general these are the offenses which the magistrate may punish by the imposition of a fine (ἐπιβολή), without referring the case to a court; this summary police jurisdiction was attached to practically all public officials and may be regarded as a survival of the judicial powers wielded by magistrates in early times. Cf. Lipsius, *Recht*, 53 ff.

[25] *Supra* 76.

attainder of treason or felony works corruption of blood.[26] Furthermore, the number and character of the Athenian courts of criminal jurisdiction tended to emphasize a division and classification of offenses that rested upon an entirely different basis. The enforcement of the criminal law was not provided for by instituting a single comprehensive jurisdiction, with inferior and superior courts, for the trial of all offenses. It was entrusted to a comparatively large number of specialized courts, each having original and exclusive jurisdiction within its province.[27] Since the presiding officials usually discharged executive as well as judicial functions, the province of a particular court was generally determined by the character of the executive duties performed by its presiding officer. Thus all offenses having to do with religion (including homicide or attempted homicide) were tried in the court of the king archon, those connected with family relationships and inheritance in the court of the archon; offenses in which aliens were concerned came before the polemarch, military offenses before the strategi; offenses against the state as a whole or against individual rights and property not otherwise provided for fell within the jurisdiction of the thesmothetes, whose court came nearest to being what we should consider a court of general criminal jurisdiction. The statutes enforced by the several courts constituted recognized divisions of the code, strictly observed in legislation[28] and therefore constantly present to the minds of the Athenians. This is the classification that would be followed instinctively by an ancient writer and has been adopted in several exhaustive and scholarly modern expositions of Attic law.[29]

[26] Stephen, *Hist. Crim. Law* I, 487.

[27] On the general character of the jurisdiction of the several magistrates, cf. Lipsius, *Recht*, 52 ff.

[28] Dem. xxiv. 20 ff.; cf. Gilbert, *Cons. Ant.*, 300 ff.

[29] E.g., *MSL* and Lipsius, *Recht*.

If it is intended, however, to give an account of Attic criminal law that may serve as an adequate basis for comparison with other systems, it would be desirable to follow the general classification of crimes according to the nature of the offense adopted in most modern treatises on criminal law.[30] This is capable of being applied with comparatively slight modification to the penal codes of many modern states, and would serve very well as the framework for a systematic exposition of the Attic law.   The various acts and omissions punished as crimes under Anglo-American and Continental law would be taken up in this general order and an endeavor made to discover how they were dealt with under the Attic law, whether by criminal or quasi-criminal actions, or by civil suit, or in both ways.   The inquiry would necessarily involve the assembling of the extant remains—unfortunately scattered and fragmentary remains—of the substantive criminal law, with some consideration of jurisdiction, forms of action, and penalties.   It would appropriately be followed by the consideration of such general doctrines as have to do with intent, malice, fraud, capacity, responsibility, etc., from the standpoint of Attic law.   At the conclusion of such a study, we should be in a position to attempt with some confidence a precise evaluation of Athenian achievement in the realm of criminal law.

[30] *Encyclopedia Britannica,* s.v. "Criminal Law."   In general this is the classification adopted by Stephen in his *History of the Criminal Law.*

BIBLIOGRAPHY

Ardaillon, E. Les mines du Laurion dans l'antiquité. Paris, 1897.

Beauchet, L. Histoire du droit privé de la république athénienne. Paris, 1897.

Bentham, J. Works (Ed. Bowring). Edinburgh, 1843.

Bonner, R. J. Administration of Justice in the Age of Hesiod. Class. Phil. VII (1912), 17–23.

————— Administration of Justice in the Age of Homer. Class. Phil. VI (1911), 12–36.

————— The Institution of Athenian Arbitrators. Class. Phil. XI (1916), 191 95.

Bréhier, L. De Graecorum iudiciorum origine. Paris, 1899.

Buck, C. D. Introduction to the Study of the Greek Dialects. Boston, 1910.

Bury, J. B. History of Greece to the Death of Alexander. London, 1904.

Busolt, G. Griechische Geschichte bis zur Schlacht bei Chaeroneia. Gotha, I, 1893; II, 1895; III¹, 1897; III², 1904.

Calhoun, G. M. Athenian Magistrates and Special Pleas. Class. Phil. XIV (1919), 338–50.

————— The Early History of Crime and Criminal Law in Greece. Proc. Class. Assoc. XVIII (1922), 86–104.

————— Ἐπίσκηψις and the δίκη ψευδομαρτυρίων. Class. Phil. XI (1916), 365–94.

————— Oral and Written Pleading in Athenian Courts. Trans. Am. Phil. Assoc. L (1919), 177–93.

Christ, W. Geschichte der griechischen Literatur. Ed. 4, Munich, 1905.

Clerc, M. Les métèques athéniens. Paris, 1893.

Comparetti, D.   Le leggi di Gortyna e le altre iscrizioni arcaiche Cretesi. Mon. Ant. III, Milan, 1893.

Craies, W. F.   Article, Criminal Law.   Encyc. Brit., ed. 11.

Croiset, A. and M.   Histoire de la littérature grecque.   I.   Paris, 1910.

Curtius, E.   Stadtgeschichte von Athen.   Berlin, 1891.

Dareste-Haussoullier-Reinach.   Recueil des inscriptions juridiques grecques. Paris, I, 1895; II, 1898–1904. Cited as *RIJG* (text) and *Recueil* (commentary).

Ehrenberg, V.   Die Rechtsidee im frühen Griechentum. Leipzig, 1921.

Fanta, A.   Der Staat in der Ilias und Odyssee.   Innsbruck, 1882.

Freeman, Kathleen.   The Work and Life of Solon.   Cardiff and London, 1926.

Gilbert, F. B.   Criminal Law and Practice of the State of New York.   Albany, 1921.

Gernet, L.   Sur l'exécution capitale.   Rev. Ét. Gr. XXXVII (1924), 261–93.

Gilbert, G.   The Constitutional Antiquities of Sparta and Athens. Tr. Nicklin and Brooks, London, 1895.

Gilliard, C.   Quelques réformes de Solon.   Lausanne, 1907.

Gillies, M. M.   Purification in Homer.   Class. Quart. XIX (1925), 71–74.

Glotz, G.   L'épistate des proèdres.   Rev. Ét. Gr. XXXIV (1921), 1–19.

——— Études sur l'antiquité grecque.   Paris, 1906.

——— La solidarité de la famille dans le droit criminel en Grèce. Paris, 1904.

Goudy, H.   Article, Roman Law.   Encyc. Brit., ed. 11.

Griffiths, A. G. F.   Article, Crime.   Encyc. Brit., ed. 11.

Grote, G.   History of Greece.   Ed. 3.   London, 1851.

Haussoullier, B.   Traité entre Delphes et Pellana.   (Bibl. Ec. Hautes Ét. 222.)   Paris, 1917.

Headlam, J. W.   The Procedure of the Gortynian Inscription. Jour. Hell. St. XIII (1892–93), 48–69.

Heffter, A. W. Die athenäische Gerichtsverfassung. Cologne, 1822.

Hirzel, R. Themis, Dike und Verwandtes. Leipzig, 1907.

Kahrstedt, U. Griechisches Staatsrecht. I. Sparta und seine Symmachie. Göttingen, 1922.

Kenny, C. S. Outlines of Criminal Law. Cambridge, 1904.

Koehler and Ziebarth. Das Stadtrecht von Gortyn und seine Beziehungen zum gemeingriechischen Rechte. Göttingen, 1912.

Leaf, Walter. Homer and History. London, 1915.

Leist, B. W. Gräco-italische Rechtsgeschichte. Jena, 1884.

Linforth, I. M. Solon the Athenian. Univ. Calif. Publ. Class. Phil. VI, Berkeley, 1919.

Lipsius, J. H. Das attische Recht und Rechtsverfahren. Leipzig, 1905–1915. Cited as *Recht*.

Lobeck, C. A. Aglaophamus. Königsberg, 1829.

Maine, H. S. Ancient Law. Am. ed., 4. New York, 1884.

Meier-Schoemann. Der attische Process. Halle, 1824.

——— Der attische Process, neu bearbeitet von J. H. Lipsius. Berlin, 1883–1887. Cited as *MSL*.

Meyer, E. Forschungen zur alten Geschichte. Halle, 1892–1899.

——— Geschichte des Alterthums. II. Stuttgart, 1893.

Mueller, K. O. Eumeniden. Göttingen, 1833.

Naegelsbach, K. F. Homerische Theologie. Nuremberg, 1884.

Neumann-Partsch. Physikalische Geographie von Griechenland. Breslau, 1885.

Perrot, G. Essai sur le droit public d'Athènes. Paris, 1867.

Philippi, A. Der Areopag und die Epheten. Berlin, 1874.

Pollock, F. A First Book of Jurisprudence. Ed., 4. London, 1918.

Pollock and Maitland. History of English Law. Cambridge, 1899.

Sanctis, G. de. ΑΤΘΙΣ. Storia della repubblica ateniese. Turin, 1912.

Sandys, J. E. History of Classical Scholarship. I. Ed. 2, Cambridge, 1906.

Schoemann, G. F. Griechische Altertümer. Ed. 4, Berlin, 1897–1902.

Scott, J. A. Homer and his Influence. Boston, 1925.

Seymour, T. D. Life in the Homeric Age. New York, 1907.

Smith, F. Athenian Political Commissions. Chicago, 1920.

Smith, Gertrude. The Administration of Justice from Hesiod to Solon. Chicago, 1924.

—— Early Greek Codes. Class. Phil. XVII (1922), 187–201.

Stephen, J. F. History of the Criminal Law of England. London, 1883.

Strachan-Davidson, J. L. Problems of the Roman Criminal Law. Oxford, 1912.

Swoboda, H. Beiträge zur griechischen Rechtsgeschichte I. Zschr. Sav. St. (Rom.) XXVI (1905), 149 ff.

Thonissen, J. J. Le droit pénal de la république athénienne. Précédé d'une étude sur le droit criminel de la Grèce légendaire. Brussels and Paris, 1875.

Treston, H. J. Poine. A Study in Ancient Greek Blood-Vengeance. London, 1923.

Ure, P. N. The Origin of Tyranny. Cambridge, 1922.

Usteri, P. Aechtung und Verbannung im griechischen Recht. Berlin, 1903.

Vinogradoff, P. Outlines of Historical Jurisprudence. London, I, 1920; II, 1922.

Ziebarth, E. Der Fluch im griechischen Recht. Hermes XXX (1895), 57–70.

Ziehen, L. Die drakontische Gesetzgebung. N. Rh. Mus. LIV (1899), 321–44.

INDEX

REGISTER OF PASSAGES

146   CRIMINAL LAW IN ANCIENT GREECE

INSCRIPTIONS